THEATRE

Art in Action

Teacher's Manual

Consultants

Reviewers

THEATRE
Art in Action

Teacher's Manual

National Textbook Company
a division of NTC/CONTEMPORARY PUBLISHING GROUP • LINCOLNWOOD, ILLINOIS USA

Cover and Interior Design: Vita Jay
Cover Photo: T. Charles Erikson/Theatre Pix

ISBN: 0–8442–5310–3

Published by National Textbook Company,
a division of NTC/Contemporary Publishing Group, Inc.
4255 West Touhy Avenue,
Lincolnwood (Chicago), Illinois 60712-1975 U.S.A.
©1999 NTC/Contemporary Publishing Group, Inc.
Manufactured in the United States of America.

90 VL09876543.

theatre—art in action

Contents

Projects

Section 2. Preparation Lessons — 55

Chapter 4. Acting — 56

Historical Profile: Shakespeare, from *A Midsummer Night's Dream* — 60

Chapter 5. Directing & Producing — 63

Historical Profile: Molière, from *Tartuffe* — 67

Chapter 6. Technical Theatre — 70

Projects

Projects

Resources   151

Using This Program

Theatre—Art in Action was created by a group of theatre educators united by their enthusiasm for introducing young people to theatre. Our development team included teachers at both the high-school and college levels, a district supervisor in theatre education, a specialist in arts therapy, and administrators at major professional theatres. We were also united by the feeling that existing theatre education materials were not very useful to either students or teachers. All these qualities—the enthusiasm, the experience, and the desire to try fresh approaches—are reflected in this program.

The most important difference between *Theatre—Art in Action* and existing programs is its far greater emphasis on performance. This emphasis grew out of a shared recognition by the development team that existing materials in theatre education seemed more concerned with *reading about* theatre than with *doing* theatre. Our basic goal in developing *Theatre—Art in Action* was to assist students in learning about theatre by offering a variety of interesting and stimulating activities and performance projects. At every stage, what students are reading is reinforced and extended with engaging things to do.

Student Text

The core of *Theatre—Art in Action* is the student text. In the student text, the emphasis on performance is reflected at three different levels—exercises, activities, and projects:

- Many exercises within the acting chapters provide immediate applications for skills the student is learning. This application is reserved for acting skills because, unlike technical theatre skills, acting skills can frequently be performed without tools and equipment, and unlike directing and producing skills, they can often be done without much preparation.

- Eight to sixteen activities at the end of each chapter deal with all of the major areas covered in the chapter. The activities can be used as in-class or homework assignments or as opportunities for extra-credit work. Most can be completed in one or two days.

- Forty large-scale projects—10 at the end of each section—will provide a broad range of creative challenges for your students. A number of these projects are also available as an alternative performance-based tool for you to use in assessing your students.

Structuring Your Course

Another important difference between *Theatre—Art in Action* and existing programs is the organization of the student text (see the chart on pp. xvi–xvii), which allows for greater flexibility in structuring your course. Three major strands deal with acting, directing and producing, and technical theatre. These strands are organized into four developmental sections: Exploration, which deals with basic tools and techniques in each of these three areas; Preparation, which gets students ready for a production; Performance, which moves through the rehearsal process to opening night and postproduction;

and Specialization, which explores various types of theatre forms and techniques. You might decide to teach each section as a unit, addressing acting, directing and producing, and technical theatre in turn. You might decide to teach the strands as units, developing each from Exploration through Specialization. Other structures and emphases, of course, are also possible.

Integrating Writing

From the playwright's first draft to the drama critic's review, writing is central to the theatre process. Far more than in other theatre programs, writing is integral to *Theatre—Art in Action*. Draw students' attention to the article at the front of their text that introduces the idea of using a Theatre Notebook. Discuss with them the value of such a notebook both in doing their performance work and as a record of their growth and discoveries as they learn about theatre. The article suggests a number of specific ways in which students might use their Theatre Notebooks, such as creating a playgoing log, and offers possible formats for various types of entries. Point out to students that throughout the text they will encounter reminders in activities and projects to include writing products and other materials in their Theatre Notebooks. Make sure that students are aware that at the back of their text is Writing & Theatre, a series of articles offering guidelines and models for basic types of theatre writing, such as plays, Reader's Theatre adaptations, promotional writing, and research papers.

Integrating Theatre History

Theatre—Art in Action also differs from existing programs in its approach to theatre history. Our development team decided that *Theatre—Art in Action* would not address theatre history in a single, isolated chapter, but teach it in an invitational, integrated fashion. At the front of the student text is a 15-page illustrated Outline of Theatre History. Suggest that students spend a few minutes exploring the outline, examining the images, getting a sense of the broad sweep of theatre history. Point out to them that many of the performance traditions, dramatic forms, theatre movements, and personalities they encounter in the outline will be discussed later in their text.

A Historical Profile follows each acting chapter and each directing and producing chapter. These profiles serve two purposes: they provide important background on major playwrights and theatre traditions, and they include a scene from a play, offering opportunities for acting or directing practice.

Linking Theatre to the Workplace

One of the most important issues involved in any area of study is its links to the world of work. What preparation is needed for various careers in theatre? What other kinds of jobs might theatre education prepare students for? *Theatre—Art in Action* helps students explore answers to these questions. When they encounter an activity in the book labeled Job Shadow, they are encouraged to take a look at a variety of careers for which theatre education could provide useful background. The program is also linked to the work world with a Careers & Theatre section at the back of the student text. This section comprises a series of profiles in which various theatre professionals talk about their jobs and how they got them.

Learning the Language of Theatre

Theatre has a highly specialized vocabulary. A list of key vocabulary terms with definitions appears at the beginning of each chapter in the student text. These key terms will be included in the chapter test. Throughout the text students will find many other boldfaced vocabulary words. Explain to them that all of these terms are defined in the Glossary at the back of their text. Stress the value of using the Glossary to clarify their understanding of technical terms.

Teacher's Manual

This *Teacher's Manual* includes lessons for each chapter, historical profile, and project in the student text. These lessons are preceded by a special section called Invitation designed to introduce students to the excitement and challenge of theatre as an art in action.

Teaching the Invitation Section

Some teachers prefer not to hand out textbooks on the first day of class, not only because students are still transferring into and out of class but also because those teachers want their students' first work to be action-based. The Invitation section describes basic hands-on interactive exercises that you can use during the first 10 days of class. The exercises are mostly theatre games that provide developmental elements for later, more complex work on acting, directing and producing, and technical theatre.

Teaching the Chapters

Each chapter lesson in this *Teacher's Manual* includes the following elements:

- The **Overview** identifies the topics, concepts, and skills covered in the chapter in the order of their appearance. It also describes how they fit into the theatre process and suggests connections to real life and other areas of the curriculum.

- **The Language of Theatre** reproduces the list of key vocabulary words that appears at the beginning of each chapter in the student text.

- A list of chapter **Objectives** identifies teaching objectives.

- A list of **Resources** identifies a variety of resources needed for the chapter. These include performance space, collections of plays, tools and supplies, and so on. It also references materials in the *Teacher's Resource Book* that you can use in teaching the chapter.

- **Customizing** provides tips for tailoring instruction to specific populations (at-risk, physically challenged, gifted, English-language learners, and so on) and shows possibilities for cooperative learning, cross-curricular connections, multicultural issues, research activities, and so on.

- **Side-Coaching Tips** help you provide ongoing support as students do activities. This support might include safety tips, advice for handling stage fright, tips on mastering various theatre techniques, and so on.

- **Support for Activities** gives guidelines for completing the chapter activities.
- **Student Assessment** identifies the assessment options provided by the program. These include a chapter test and a rubric for using one of the projects as an alternative, performanced-based assessment tool.

Teaching the Historical Profiles

The historical profile lesson includes the same elements as the chapter lesson, except that **Support for Activities** is replaced with **Alternative Activities**, which lists activities that you could use as opportunities for extra-credit work or as a substitute for the activities suggested at the end of each profile.

Teaching the Projects

Each project lesson includes the following elements:

- The **Assignment** identifies the product or performance that is the outcome of the project.
- A list of project **Objectives** identifies teaching objectives.
- A list of **Resources** includes what is necessary or helpful to complete the project. It also references materials in the *Teacher's Resource Book* that students can use in completing the project.
- **Creating** provides tips you can use to help students complete their projects.
- **Performing/Presenting** gives tips you can use to help students perform or present their projects.
- **Responding** discusses different ways in which you and your students can assess their projects.

Assessing Your Students

Theatre—Art in Action emphasizes performance-based assessment. The article on pages xxii–xxvi of this *Teacher's Manual* discusses using and developing rubrics for assessment, provides guidelines, and offers a variety of sample rubrics. For each chapter, a project is identified as an appropriate alternative performance-based assessment. For these projects, rubrics are included in the *Teacher's Resource Book*. The program also provides standard assessment tools in the form of chapter and historical profile tests covering key vocabulary terms and concepts.

National Standards for Theatre Education

The result of the Goals 2000: Educate America Act was to place theatre, with the other arts, in the core curriculum, alongside math and English. Since 1992, arts educators have collaborated on the National Standards for Arts Education. The National Standards for Theatre Education were developed by The American Alliance for Theatre and Education (AATE) with the cooperation of the Educational Theatre Association (ETA). These standards were not written as a comprehensive course of study, but as a challenge to theatre educators to develop teaching strategies that would lead to competency, proficiency, and excellence in theatre at all grade levels.

During the process of developing, creating, and refining *Theatre—Art in Action,* every effort was taken to meet or exceed all aspects of the National Standards for Theatre Education for grades 9–12. (These standards appear in the Resources section of this *Teacher's Manual* on pages 172–176.) Some of the exercises, activities, projects, and profiles were constructed to assist the teacher in helping their students fully realize the intent of the standards. Others were designed as springboards for deeper exploration, examination, and experimentation of a benchmark standard by the students, both individually and collaboratively. The teacher as a facilitator can easily use this text as a tool to mentor their students to reach and surpass these high standards, which have been endorsed nationally.

Teacher's Resource Book

Your *Teacher's Resource Book* offers 164 blackline masters and 26 overhead transparencies. The blackline masters include chapter tests on concepts and vocabulary terms, historical profile tests, alternative assessment rubrics, research activities, and a variety of additional support materials in the areas of acting, directing and producing, technical theatre, writing, careers, theatre safety, and other areas. The overheads include a variety of instructional diagrams as well as 12 reproductions of fine art used in theatre activities keyed to each chapter.

Emergency Activity Cards

Imagine that you have the flu or jury duty or you are taking members of another class to perform at a theatre festival. What do you do for your substitute? A special feature of *Theatre—Art in Action* is the inclusion of 8 Emergency Activity Cards with 32 activities designed for substitute teachers. These cards provide a variety of additional individual and small group activities that are keyed to each strand and section; substitutes will therefore give students activities that are appropriate for their skills and development in the course thus far. You will find the cards in the binder pocket of your *Teacher's Resource Book.*

Technical Theatre Videotape

Shot at the Theatre School at DePaul University in Chicago, *The Production Process* is an approximately 23-minute videotape that uses an engaging narrative format to give your students a first-hand, real-life look at technical theatre preparation. The tape features interviews with theatre personnel as they work backstage during the technical rehearsals of a production of Molière's *The Imaginary Invalid.*

Books of Scenes and Monologues

The scenes included in the historical profiles in the student text are supplemented by two separate collections: *The Book of Scenes for*

Aspiring Actors is a collection of scenes from a variety of plays, all of which feature young characters. *The Book of Monologues for Aspiring Actors* is a collection of excerpts from plays featuring young characters. Playwrights range from Sophocles and Molière to David Henry Hwang and Laura Harrington.

A Parting Word

Theatre is basic to a balanced, academic, educational experience for all students. The diversity of *Theatre—Art in Action* provides opportunities for the involvement of all students regardless of experience and abilities. These exercises, activities, profiles, and projects promote unity, inquiry, critical and constructive thought, as well as skills of comparison, problem-solving, interpretation, judgment, and research. Students are encouraged to investigate old and new ideas by exploring, discovering, creating, and clarifying their perceptions and knowledge.

Theatre education is a creative and critical-thinking process that helps students foster a healthy self-concept, develop intrapersonal skills, clarify their perceptions of the world, and nurture an awareness of themselves as physical, social, and creative beings. Students are encouraged to develop interpersonal skills, cultivate empathy for others, explore relationships, and enhance real-world communication skills.

Theatre—Art in Action is aimed at promoting active lifelong learners; encouraging broad, worldwide views; embracing technology and multimedia; nurturing alternative ways of knowing and learning; and serving the widely divergent needs of all students. The program was designed to utilize a variety of standard and authentic assessment strategies. An emphasis on linking hands-on knowledge to real-world situations and workplace skills is embedded within this program, along with the flexibility for adapting the materials to accommodate diverse learning styles and needs. The goal of *Theatre—Art in Action* is that students will discover their creativity through performing, writing, designing, constructing, and evaluating. Our hope is that students become artists, technicians, and evaluators as they acquire an understanding of theatre.

Rob Taylor
Bob Strickland

Theatre—Art in Action

Program Components

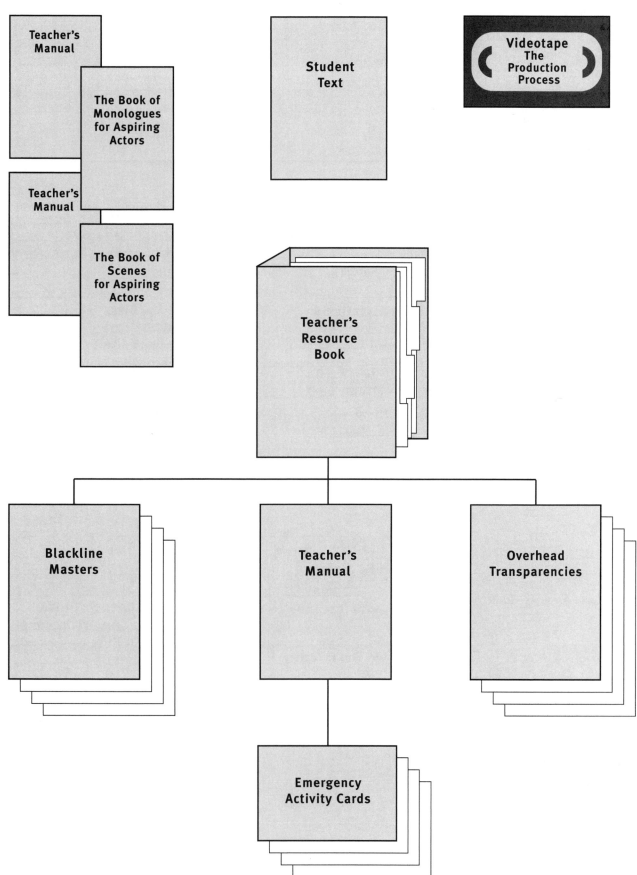

Teacher's Manual

The Book of Monologues for Aspiring Actors

Teacher's Manual

The Book of Scenes for Aspiring Actors

Student Text

Videotape
The Production Process

Teacher's Resource Book

Blackline Masters

Teacher's Manual

Overhead Transparencies

Emergency Activity Cards

Organization of Student Text

	Exploration	Preparation	
Using a Theatre Notebook • Getting Started • Playgoing Log • Acting Notes • Directing & Producing Notes • Technical Theatre Notes	**Chapter 1. Acting** • Self-Awareness • Movement • Pantomime • Voice • Improvisation • Storytelling **Activities**	**Chapter 4. Acting** • The Characterization Process • Motivation and Behavior • Creating a Specific Character • Stage Movement Basics • Auditions **Activities**	
An Outline of Theatre History	**Historical Profile:** The Storytelling Tradition, from *Sundiata, an Epic of Old Mali*	**Historical Profile:** Shakespeare, from *A Midsummer Night's Dream*	
	Chapter 2. Directing & Producing • The Roles of Director and Producer • The Production Team • The Performance Space **Activities**	**Chapter 5. Directing & Producing** • Choosing a Play • Genre • Working with the Script • Style • The Director's Role in Design • Stage Composition • Blocking • The Director's Promptbook • The Business of the Play • The Stage Manager **Activities**	
	Historical Profile: Sophocles, from *Antigone*	**Historical Profile:** Molière, from *Tartuffe*	
	Chapter 3. Technical Theatre • The Stage Crew • Set Construction and Prop Crews • Lighting and Sound Crews • Costume and Makeup Crews **Activities**	**Chapter 6. Technical Theatre** • Emergence of the Design Team • Elements of Effective Production Design • Set Design • Set Construction • Joining, Bracing, and Stiffening Scenery • Painting Scenery • Prop Design and Construction • Lighting Design • Sound Design and Production • Costume Design and Production • Makeup Design **Activities**	
xvi	Projects	Projects	

Additional Program Resources

The chart below is a guide to the additional resources available in the *Teacher's Resource Book*. Opposite each chapter, historical profile, and project in the student text are listed the numbers of all the blackline masters (BLM) and overhead transparencies (OVH) in the *Teacher's Resource Book* that relate to it. The chart also lists the blackline masters that can be used in conjunction with the Invitation section in the *Teacher's Manual*.

Teacher's Manual	Teacher's Resource Book	
	BLM #	OVH #
Invitation	1, 2, 3, 4, 5, 139, 140	
Student Text		
Section 1. Exploration		
Chapter 1. Acting	1, 2, 3, 4, 5, 7, 8, 9, 10, 11, 12, 13, 14, 103, 123, 127, 139, 140, 157, 158, 163, 164	1, 2, 15
Historical Profile: The Storytelling Tradition, from *Sundiata, an Epic of Old Mali*	13, 14, 115, 123, 139, 140, 141, 142	
Chapter 2. Directing & Producing	1, 3, 4, 5, 6, 7, 35, 36, 37, 104, 123, 128, 139, 140, 159, 160, 163, 164	3, 4, 5, 6, 7, 8, 16
Historical Profile: Sophocles, from *Antigone*	116, 123, 139, 140, 143, 144	
Chapter 3. Technical Theatre	1, 3, 4, 5, 6, 7, 57, 58, 59, 60, 61, 62, 63, 93, 105, 123, 129, 139, 140, 161, 162, 163, 164	17
Project 1: Telling a Story	9, 10, 13, 14, 127, 139, 140	
Project 2: Animal Pantomime	9, 10, 63, 64, 139, 140	
Project 3: Improvisation and Tableau	9, 10, 11, 12, 139, 140	
Project 4: Soundscapes	63, 64, 139, 140	
Project 5: Perspectives on Theatre Spaces	37, 139, 140	
Project 6: Analyzing Theatre Spaces	128, 139, 140	
Project 7: Building a Model Stage	57, 139, 140	
Project 8: Shop Inventory	139, 140	
Project 9: Sewing Demonstration Board	139, 140	
Project 10: Makeup Scrapbook	129, 139, 140	
Section 2. Preparation		
Chapter 4. Acting	8, 9, 10, 11, 15, 16, 17, 18, 19, 20, 21, 22, 23, 24, 25, 26, 106, 124, 130, 139, 140, 157, 158, 163, 164	9, 10, 18

Teacher's Resource Book

Student Text	BLM #	OVH #
Historical Profile: Shakespeare, from *A Midsummer Night's Dream*	117, 124, 139, 140, 145, 146	13
Chapter 5. Directing & Producing	6, 38, 39, 40, 41, 42, 43, 44, 45, 46, 47, 48, 107, 124, 131, 139, 140, 159, 160, 163, 164	6, 7, 8, 19
Historical Profile: Molière, from *Tartuffe*	118, 124, 139, 140, 147, 148	
Chapter 6. Technical Theatre	6, 57, 59, 61, 63, 64, 65, 66, 67, 68, 69, 70, 71, 72, 73, 74, 75, 76, 77, 78, 79, 80, 81, 82, 83, 84, 85, 86, 87, 88, 89, 90, 91, 92, 93, 108, 124, 132, 139, 140, 161, 162, 163, 164	11, 20
Project 11: Open Dialogue with Stage Movement	9, 10, 11, 19, 20, 21, 22, 23, 24, 25, 26, 139, 140	
Project 12: Building Characters	9, 10, 19, 20, 21, 22, 23, 24, 25, 26, 130, 139, 140	
Project 13: Delivering a Monologue	9, 10, 19, 20, 21, 22, 23, 24, 25, 26, 139, 140	
Project 14: Entrances and Exits	9, 10, 19, 20, 21, 22, 23, 24, 25, 26, 139, 140	
Project 15: Creating Stage Pictures	15, 131, 139, 140	
Project 16: Developing a Director's Promptbook	38, 39, 40, 41, 42, 43, 44, 45, 139, 140	
Project 17: Producing a Play	49, 139, 140	
Project 18: Designing a Set	63, 64, 65, 66, 77, 78, 79, 80, 81, 83, 84, 91, 92, 132, 139, 140	
Project 19: Reupholstering a Set Prop	57, 139, 140	
Project 20: Grid Transfer	57, 72, 139, 140	
Section 3. Performance		
Chapter 7. Acting	9, 10, 11, 15, 16, 17, 18, 19, 20, 21, 22, 23, 24, 25, 26, 27, 28, 29, 30, 31, 32, 109, 125, 133, 139, 140, 157, 158, 163, 164	21
Historical Profile: Kabuki, from *The Zen Substitute*	119, 125, 139, 140, 149, 150	14
Chapter 8. Directing & Producing	38, 39, 40, 41, 42, 43, 44, 45, 49, 50, 51, 52, 53, 54, 55, 56, 110, 125, 134, 139, 140, 159, 160, 163, 164	12, 22

Student Text	Teacher's Resource Book	
	BLM #	OVH #
Project 33: Staging a Fight	2, 41, 42, 139, 140	
Project 34: Acting On-Camera	9, 10, 19, 20, 21, 22, 23, 24, 25, 26, 27, 28, 29, 30, 45, 139, 140	
Project 35: Directing a Reader's Theatre Piece	39, 40, 41, 42, 43, 44, 45, 55, 56, 137, 139, 140	
Project 36: Developing a Musical	33, 34, 39, 40, 41, 42, 43, 44, 45, 49, 51, 52, 53, 55, 56, 139, 140	
Project 37: Three-Dimensional Scenery	57, 139, 140	
Project 38: Projecting a Background	59, 139, 140	
Project 39: Creating Jewelry	61, 139, 140	
Project 40: Making a Mask	102, 138, 139, 140	

Using Rubrics to Assess Student Projects

By Bill Peery, Bob Strickland, and Rob Taylor

A well-designed rubric provides a set of criteria that enables a teacher to assess and validate levels of student performance. Through a means of self-assessment, rubrics provide students with necessary information about what they need to do to excel. Involving students in the evaluation process gives them an increased sense of responsibility for and ownership of their work. Setting forth at the outset criteria that constitute excellence in a finished product enables students to answer the perennial question, "Am I doing a good job?" Rubrics also provide a uniform rating system for all students in a class, establishing a range of performance standards, from maximum to minimum, based on a set of standardized criteria. In so doing, rubrics provide students, teachers, and parents with grades that are more meaningful than those provided by more traditional grading systems.

The development of any rubric must begin with a clearly stated purpose, or objective. What do you as the teacher expect students to accomplish through an activity? In the case of the projects in this text, a product and a purpose—a what and a why—are provided in the Project Planner at the start of each project. While you may never state product and purpose on your finished rubric, these will provide a basis for the assessment criteria you develop.

There are three basic components to any rubric:

- **Criteria** These are the items upon which an activity will be evaluated.

- **Descriptors** There is a descriptor for each criterion. These descriptors define the expectations for each criterion.

- **Achievement Levels** These define the range of choices for evaluation or the "levels of excellence and/or proficiency." When initially constructing rubrics, make sure that you first develop criteria to describe terms such as "excellent" or "competent" before attaching these levels to your rubric.

Project Planners at the beginning of each project provide students with a set of specifications, called Specs, to guide them through the project by providing the tasks necessary for completion. These tasks for project completion can be used as a basis for developing rubric scoring criteria and descriptors for each project.

Below are achievement levels and definitions for descriptors for a five-point rubric:

5 **Excellent** Demonstrates excellence in all aspects of the work performed, with all specifications fully accomplished to maximum quality standards.

4 **Proficient** Demonstrates an excellent level of achievement in the majority of the work performed with most specification criteria accomplished to maximum quality.

3 **Competent** Demonstrates good quality performance in all working specifications. This represents the level that all students should be capable of achieving.

2 **Adequate** Demonstrates a moderate display of performance in most working specifications without fully achieving all Competent levels. Students at this level may display some difficulty in the completion of tasks.

1 **Unsatisfactory** Demonstrates minimal levels in all working specifications. Displays a lack of understanding of concepts and difficulty in the completion of all or most tasks.

Sample rubrics follow for three of the projects in the text. These samples are intended to provide you with ideas for constructing rubrics of your own. There is no such thing as a perfect rubric; rubrics undergo constant modification. Rubrics will and should change to meet the needs of various groups of students and teachers. You may choose to use these sample rubrics as they are or to adapt them to meet your current classroom needs.

Sample Rubric
Project 7: Building a Model Stage

Project Criteria	Excellent	Proficient	Competent	Adequate	Unsatisfactory
Scale	Meets criteria for Proficient and includes surrounding areas, such as lobby or dressing rooms, to scale.	Meets criteria for Competent and includes preliminary sketches.	Scale is accurate to actual theatre measurements.	Measurements are in evidence but inaccurate.	Scale measures not used or are very inaccurate.
Theatre Space and Details	Meets criteria for Proficient and adds details such as proscenium arch, orchestra pit, and curtains.	Meets criteria for Competent and includes details relevant to theatre space, such as surrounding rooms.	Includes relevant/ pertinent areas of theatre space.	Relevant areas not included or are inaccurately represented.	Model shows little resemblance to the actual theatre.
Appropriate Medium	Meets criteria for Proficient and includes such things as real fabric for curtains.	Meets criteria for Competent and strengthens weak points, such as back wall and proscenium arch.	Model is constructed of appropriate material, such as sturdy cardboard or balsa wood.	Uses lightweight material for construction. Structure is not adequately supported.	Construction work shows very little effort.
Production	Meets criteria for Proficient and is painted with additional colors used for curtains, proscenium arch, and orchestra pit.	Meets criteria for Competent and lines are straight, corners are sharp. No visible glue smears.	Work is neat and shows careful attention to details.	Lines are uneven, corners are not sharp, glue smears are evident.	Overall effect of project is of one hastily thrown together.

Sample Rubric
Project 14: Entrances and Exits

Project Criteria	Excellent	Proficient	Competent	Adequate	Unsatisfactory
Character Creation	Creates a believable character that is very detailed in delivery and execution.	Meets the criteria for Competent and maintains focus throughout.	Establishes a believable character through clearly visible actions.	Creates a character that is not believable.	Shows little evidence of character creation.
Character Attributes	Meets criteria for Proficient and blends attributes together in creating a character.	Clearly portrays at least two character attributes, such as physical and mental.	Clearly portrays at least one major physical, mental, or emotional attribute of character.	Communication of character attributes is awkward and not fully developed.	Communication of attributes shows little change from performer's own actions.
Character Interaction	Interactions at entrance and exit seem natural and involve more than one other character.	Interaction with another character develops strong stage entrance and exit.	Stage interactions at entrance and exit are obvious and understandable.	Stage interactions at entrance and exit are difficult to comprehend.	Stage entrance and exit are weak and unfocused.
Performance	Dramatizes the scene with appropriate and dramatically interesting ideas.	Easily assumes characterization in performance.	Works well in ensemble and is comfortable with characterization in performance.	Is self-conscious in role and not an effective ensemble member.	Shows little interest in performing scene as a member of an ensemble.

Sample Rubric
Project 26: Directing a One-Act Play

Project Criteria	Excellent	Proficient	Competent	Adequate	Unsatisfactory
Preparatory Activities	Meets criteria for Proficient. In addition, promptbook shows a thorough and original analysis of the play. Develops an interesting and original production.	Meets criteria for Competent and keeps detailed notes on all phases of preparation.	Completes all prep work: chooses and analyzes play, develops production concept, designs ground plan, develops rehearsal schedule and budget, auditions and casts show.	Does not complete all necessary prep work prior to rehearsals.	Does little prep work beyond casting the play.
Rehearsals	Meets criteria for Proficient and works with individual actors as necessary to develop believable characters.	Meets criteria for Competent and communicates expectations to actors, resulting in detailed focus.	Conducts rehearsals in timely fashion. Communicates expectations to actors. Completes promptbook.	Sometimes fails to communicate expectations to actors. Completes promptbook haphazardly.	Fails to communicate ideas and expectations to actors. Cancels or cuts short rehearsals.
Tech Work	Meets criteria for Proficient and becomes directly involved with tech when necessary.	Meets criteria for Competent and provides a clear direction to tech staff of production concept.	Provides technical support necessary for production. Holds planning meetings with tech staff.	Sometimes fails to follow through with tech staff planning meetings.	Rarely follows through in planning meetings with tech staff or with teacher.
Performance	Meets criteria for Proficient and incorporates dramatically interesting and original ideas	Meets criteria for Competent and performance shows the result of effective rehearsal with careful attention to details.	Demonstrates directing skills through effective use of blocking, stage pictures, and character development. Shows thorough understanding of the play.	Demonstrates a partial realization of blocking, stage pictures, and character development. Shows misunderstanding of the play.	Demonstrates limited realization of blocking, stage pictures, and character development. Shows little understanding of the play.

Adapting Theatrical Productions

By Leslie Holland

Often we approach the production process in theatre with excitement and enthusiasm—until we discover that our pocket doesn't quite meet the needs of our passion. The issue of adequate funding plagues not only schools but community theatres and professional companies as well. Theatre can be expensive, and the price tag for producing theatre is costly, particularly since our school boards are feeling the effects of over-taxing, the fate of the National Endowment for the Arts itself lies in the balance, and funding for the arts in general is in jeopardy. Added to the challenge of securing continued support for producing and sustaining the arts is the sobering reality that funding agencies and individuals often use their dollars to influence the artistic product. Amazingly, theatre endures and shows still go on despite financial hurdles. What impact funding constraints will have on theatre in the near future is a source of debate, but somehow theatre will survive.

One way to survive is to adapt productions to current resources, including a limited budget. The genesis of the adaptation process, in fact, is often predicated on a theatre's budget and revenue figures from the previous year. Let's say, for example, that last season your school produced two shows: one show featured a small cast and was staged on a single set; the other was a large-scale musical. If you anticipate presenting similar shows this season, you can predict what your budget will be, and then work within those boundaries.

Continuing the example, let's say you have decided to produce Shakespeare's *A Midsummer Night's Dream* instead of a musical. You know that this selection will satisfy a two-fold mission for arts and education: it is a literary work of merit that meets statewide requirements in language arts and fine arts, and it combines the resources of your English and drama departments. Like a musical, it offers a significant number of students the opportunity to work on the production as actors, musicians, designers, and members of the tech crew. The next step is to secure any necessary rights to produce the play. Since Shakespearean plays are in the public domain, you can move on and address the technical elements of the production, including scenery, props, lighting, sound, costumes, and makeup. These technical elements of a production often stretch budgeted dollars, even with careful planning.

How can you anticipate concerns surrounding the potential of limited resources without compromising the production concept, or vision? Your first response should be to put forth an innovative and versatile vision. If the vision incorporates the dynamics of your existing theatre space into the leitmotif of the design, you can gain even more budget mileage.

The Performance Space

The central action of *A Midsummer Night's Dream* takes place in the woods, with secondary scenes in a court in Athens. The court also plays host to various theatrical conventions, such as a "play within a play" and a "double wedding ceremony." Building the design around the primary action in the woods seems the simplest and most logical choice. In this way, any additional scenes between the young lovers lost in the woods, the fairies who bewitch them, and the traveling band of performers can all take place within the proximity of the woods. Not only does this decision alleviate certain budgetary concerns but it also helps to unify the staging.

Sets, Props, and Costumes

You can approach set pieces, props, and costumes with similar resourcefulness. Inexpensive set pieces and props, such as a large chair with a "royal bearing" and a velveteen throw, can help suggest an Athenian court. Costumes accented with a regal flair can serve a dual purpose: to establish character and accentuate the environment. This creative flexibility can be applied to the woodland scenes as well: leotards and tights, sweat shirts and jogging pants could be dyed, painted, and texturized to reflect the woods motif. Frayed pieces of cloth could be attached to outer garments to suggest tree moss or branches, or to effect the ethereal quality of the fairies.

For more specific prop and costume demands, you can look to your colleagues in professional and community theatres; they will often loan items with a returnable deposit, provided the items are returned undamaged. Thrift stores and garage sales are a designer's gold mine, where set, prop, and costume pieces can be acquired at bargain basement prices. Another resource is the performers themselves, who may volunteer to use their own clothing if compensated by a rental fee and/or the producer's assurance that the items will be professionally cleaned after use.

Sound

Advances in technology have contributed to the excitement—and costs—of sound design. Having access to a high-tech studio is desirable but not always possible, especially if you are trying to cut costs. One solution for stimulating background sound is to generate an organic soundscape. Working with the sound designer, the actors can create a sort of soundtrack by combining their voices with the use of objects employed to produce specific sound effects. A soundscape for your production of *A Midsummer Night's Dream,* for example, might include actors vocalizing the sounds of crickets, frogs, birds, even the ethereal flourish of fairies. With objects they can create sounds such as thunder, the galloping of horses, or the clashing of weapons.

When musical accompaniment is required, enlisting the help of a musical director is essential. Besides determining the instrumentation, composition, and the vocal score, a musical director may also advise you on the best way to amplify sound in your theatre. When resources are restrictive, a musical director can adjust the composition and instrumentation accordingly to suit the performers. Musical directors are the best resource for finding other musicians, coordinating equipment rental, and arranging offsite rehearsals. The quality and aptitude of your musicians are also crucial. Having a well-versed percussionist, keyboard player, and reed or horn player who can command several instruments is not only ideal but practical as well. Apprentices, such as college and high-school students or nonunion musicians, are well suited for high-school musical engagements. They are usually eager, motivated, and willing to use the opportunity to develop their skills, build their resumés, and gain experience.

Lighting

Like sound, lighting design has made terrific strides in this age of computerized techno-spectacle. Slide projections, cycloramas, even disco balls are all heavily in demand, but on a small production budget they may not be attainable. Your computer lighting board and lighting instrument stock may have its limits too. Again, you might be able to borrow or rent lights from an area theatre or university theatre department, although the cost of rental can be steep. The best-case scenario is a lighting designer who can create visual effects through careful combinations of color and pattern, using gels, gobos, and existing instruments. By working in tandem with the set, sound, and costume designers, the lighting designer can achieve a unique, stylized version of your desired lighting requirements.

Stylizing

Stylizing a production is another way to defray costs. This technique may be as simple as setting the play in another time and place, updating a production to the modern day, or adopting conventions of theatrical styles from certain periods—all of which can enhance the text by revising the playwright's perspective. For your production of *A Midsummer Night's Dream,* for example, you could stylize it to take place in a modern art gallery instead of the woods. The Athenian court might be a Renoir exhibit; the young lovers might be curators or patrons at the gallery; the fairies might be spirits of the people in the paintings; and the band of traveling performers might be the gallery's security staff.

The Director and the Adaptation

The task of adaptation presents an infinite number of options as well as challenges when the creative process is influenced by your budget as well as your staging. Although the challenges may appear daunting, the payoff is rewarding, especially for whoever is willing to accept the tremendous responsibility—namely, the director. Paramount to the process of adapting a production is a visionary director capable of galvanizing the synergy of actors, designers, and tech crews in a supportive and nurturing environment. With the director's guidance, the journey of adaptation can result in an original and inventive production inspiring to both the students involved in presenting the production and the audience who enjoys it.

Invitation

Some teachers prefer not to hand out textbooks on the first day of class, not only because students are still transferring into and out of class but also because those teachers want their students' first work to be action-based. (If your curriculum is structured so that you *do* involve students with textbook assignments on the first day of class, see Chapter 1 Acting on page 24 of this *Teacher's Manual.*) The Invitation section of the program functions as an introduction to the excitement and challenge of theatre as an art in action. It describes basic hands-on exercises for the first 10 days of a theatre class. The exercises mostly take the form of theatre games that provide developmental elements for later, more complex work on acting, directing and producing, and technical theatre. Some of these exercises may be recognized by experienced theatre teachers as "oldies, but goodies," while others are newer, some modified from exercises circulating in the educational theatre arena, which encourages such sharing of ideas.

The exercises are designed to collectively address the following six key developmental elements:

- **Ensemble-building**—building cooperation as a group
- **Trust**—building confidence in each other
- **Observation**—building awareness of the immediate environment
- **Self-confidence**—building self-awareness
- **Concentration**—building a sense of attention to detail
- **Imagination and creativity**—building awareness of the art of theatre

Over the course of the 10 days, students will participate in more than 40 exercises. Some types of exercises, such as name games, are repeated in more than one lesson where such repetition seems beneficial; however, no game is repeated exactly. Although many are deceptively simple, theatre games lay the foundation for the discipline to follow. The ultimate goal of these 10 days of exercises is to get each student to the point at which he or she can begin to work effectively—individually and as part of a collaborative team—on specific exercises and activities in acting, directing and producing, and technical theatre that will eventually lead to creative performance projects.

The exercises for each day have been planned for standard 50-minute class periods and include time for evaluation and feedback during each session. For teachers who are new to the drama classroom, the exercises for each day are best followed precisely. Experienced teachers should feel free to adapt the exercises as they see fit.

Objectives

A list of overall objectives for the exercises is provided below. Each day's lesson addresses some of these objectives. Several objectives may be addressed in one exercise.

- The student will be able to demonstrate an understanding of basic developmental elements—ensemble-building, trust, observation, self-confidence, concentration, and imagination and creativity.
- The student will be able to demonstrate a working knowledge of theatre safety rules and classroom etiquette by performing tasks in accordance with established criteria.
- The student will be able to develop a sense of personal awareness.
- The student will be able to develop a language of physical expression.
- The student will be able to develop a sense of logical progression in performed narrative.
- The student will become more aware of language, speech, rhythm, movement, creativity, and imagination—both individually and within the group dynamic.
- The student will be able to demonstrate flexibility and adaptability through imaginative responses to sounds, language, and action of others.
- The student will be able to use the body and voice for creative self-expression in thought, feeling, and character.
- The student will be able to demonstrate the creative uses of theatrical transformation with respect to props and situations.
- The student will be able to use theatre games to demonstrate the ability to suspend disbelief.
- The student will be able to develop the ability to join with and respond to others in theatrical activities.
- The student will be able to develop and recognize the importance of trust as it affects actor communication.
- The student will be able to develop sensitivity to others in space, movement, and timing.
- The student will be able to recognize that theatrical collaboration respects artistic compromise.
- The student will be able to use constructive criticism to improve his or her work.
- The student will be able to interact with peers fully, imaginatively, and reflectively.
- The student will be able to demonstrate the ability to concentrate by focusing on the material being discussed, experienced, viewed, and so on.
- The student will be able to work alone and with others, with or without direct supervision.
- The student will be able to respect group decisions.
- The student will be able to demonstrate responsible behavior when participating as an audience member.

Resources

- Large open space; nonconcrete flooring; at least 2 square feet per student
- Index cards
- Various simple household or classroom objects
- Tray with a cloth cover
- Blindfold
- Soccer ball, football, or volleyball
- Tape or CD player with assorted music recordings
- Drawing of a bomb
- Wet cloth
- Assorted newspaper or magazine articles
- Assorted designs from magazines, fabric swatches, and wallpaper samples
- BLM 1 General Theatre Safety
- BLM 2 Movement Safety
- BLM 3 Backstage Etiquette
- BLM 4 Audience Etiquette
- BLM 5 Production Contract
- BLMs 139, 140 Student Self-Assessment

Student Participation

The exercises in this section are designed to work with the participation of all students. In most exercises, every student must be engaged in the exercise; there is no audience. To keep the exercises moving and make them work most effectively, therefore, be diligent about making sure that all students are involved and that no one is holding back—or being held back by others. The suggestions below will help you accomplish this objective.

Encouraging Participation

Monitor participation in preparation and performance by moving about the classroom. For students who appear not to be participating, draw them out in a natural way, asking them specific questions or making constructive comments.

Handling Stage Fright

Some students may be shy or suffer from stage fright. Allow students to work and perform first in pairs and small groups rather than individually to help alleviate these natural fears. Remind students that for theatre games, there are no mistakes. Don't ever tell a student that it's silly or stupid to feel frightened; instead, offer timely positive reinforcement (without drawing attention to the student in such a way as to embarrass the student), and make yourself available to students who want to talk one-on-one about issues of stage fright.

Improving Body Image

Many of the exercises involve movement in ways that will require students to expand their typical range of motion and style of moving. Some students may feel shy or inadequate about their bodies. Encourage them to become comfortable with their bodies—no matter the size or shape—and to respect themselves and each other as they prepare their bodies for the active work of theatre. Stress that doing theatre does not require a perfect body but one that is healthy and responsive.

Encountering Resistance

Most students should enjoy the physical activity of theatre games. Some may be reluctant to join in because they consider the games silly. Point out that every serious athlete undergoes training that includes physical warm-up exercises in order to perform well. These games should be considered calisthenics for the voice and body.

Students with Physical Disabilities

Engage students with physical disabilities in the physical exercises that they are capable of performing. Some may need longer periods of time or more individual attention. During some of the more active exercises, you might consider pairing these students with others who are willing and able to assist them if they need or want help moving around the classroom.

Classroom Management

Grouping

Many of these games are designed for small-group work. Before beginning the exercises on Day 1, establish your methods for breaking the class into these smaller units, such as counting-off. At this stage it's better for you to form the groups rather than allow students to choose teams or partners, which holds the inherent danger of having some students left out. Form different groups for each day or each exercise.

Focusing

Train students from the beginning to give you their undivided attention immediately when you call for it. You might use a coach's whistle or call "Focus on me!" This is particularly important during days in which many different exercises are scheduled.

Student Etiquette and Responsibilities

To ensure a positive, nurturing, and cooperative environment, students must respect each other. Many of the exercises are aimed at fostering an attitude of cooperation and generating a feeling of trust and support. Before beginning any exercises, it's advisable that you inform students of their responsibilities toward these goals and of your expectations for classroom etiquette.

Below are some general guidelines for student etiquette and responsibility that you may wish to pass on to your students. Some teachers make a formal contract specifying the rules of classroom etiquette and ask students to sign the contract; this can help to make students accountable for their attitudes and actions.

Students should agree to do the following to ensure a general climate of respect and responsibility:

- arrive on time for all classes
- arrive ready for work at all times
- do their best in all activities, exercises, and projects
- show respect for classmates and the teacher
- be sensitive to the needs of others
- support the creativity of others
- work as a team member
- complete all assignments on time
- treat the classroom and theatre spaces, as well as any equipment and supplies, with respect and responsibility
- follow all safety rules at all times
- follow all school and classroom rules at all times

Doing good work in theatre games means throwing oneself into the activities with sincerity and enthusiasm. Insist that students take these games seriously; there is no room for personal agendas, such as showing off or teasing another student in the group. This is particularly important during trust exercises.

After you have completed the exercises and before opening the student text, you may wish to distribute BLM 3, BLM 4, and BLM 5, which outline a number of other student rules and responsibilities they will be expected to understand and abide by during the course.

Student Safety

Safety of students is always an important concern. It becomes particularly relevant in the theatre classroom and performance spaces, where potentially dangerous equipment and supplies will be handled and where students will be experimenting with new movement and voice exercises. One way to introduce students to these special safety concerns is through BLM 1 and BLM 2. Hand these out on Day 1 and discuss any questions students may have. Ask students to keep a copy for themselves. Post a copy of each in your classroom.

Dressing for Physical Activity

Before beginning the exercises each day, check to see that students are dressed appropriately. They should wear loose-fitting clothing that permits freedom of movement. Tight-fitting and overly baggy clothing impede movement; the latter also prevents observation of possible movement or breathing problems or of excessive muscle tension. The best footwear is soft-soled shoes or gym shoes. Don't let students exercise on tile or polished wood floors in their stocking feet; there is danger of slipping. Make sure students remove necklaces, bracelets, heavy belts, and any other jewelry or accessories that might hinder or harm themselves or others during the exercises. By checking each day, students will become more conscientious and will be reminded of the need for appropriate dress.

Working at a Safe Pace

Most exercises will go smoothly and at an appropriate, safe pace only if the class cooperates in a disciplined, focused manner, observing all rules and concentrating throughout. Pacing of many exercises must be carefully managed: some exercises can and should be done quickly, even picking up speed; others need to be done slowly and deliberately.

Music can help with pacing. Many of the exercises can be done to music; some require the use of music. Upbeat music is helpful for keeping vigorous movements steady and consistent; soft, relaxing music will facilitate smooth, connected movement.

The trust exercises are designed to add complexity from lesson to lesson and are, therefore, likely to require more attention to safety as they progress. Don't rush the trust exercises or take them out of sequence.

Ensuring Proper Technique

Throughout physical activities, movements should be fluid, never jerky. Using the guidelines on BLM 2, monitor students to ensure proper techniques and to make sure they are practicing proper breathing. Warn students not to force any movement and to particularly avoid "crunching" their necks on any general warm-ups, such as neck rolls. Remind them to breathe deeply, which brings necessary oxygen to working muscles, keeps the body relaxed, and aids concentration.

Student Assessment

Your overall assessment of each student's progress may be accomplished by measuring achievement of the objectives outlined at the beginning of this section. Students may demonstrate their success at meeting those objectives through participation in the exercises.

Student Self-Assessment

Each day's exercises include time for evaluation and feedback. On Day 1, you should explain to students that you will engage them in self-evaluation at the end of each of the 10 class periods and that you will be assessing them throughout the Invitation exercises on their growth in the areas of the six developmental elements (p. 1). BLMs 139 and 140 provide questions that will help students in written or oral self-assessment as well.

Self-assessment is integral to student progress in *Theatre—Art in Action*. Questions are peppered throughout the text, and each of the 40 projects includes a number of self-assessment questions. In addition, the student text will introduce students to the use of the Theatre Notebook (p. xx). You may wish to have students save any written self-assessment they do during these Invitation exercises so that they may include it in their Theatre Notebooks later.

Element Assessment Questions

In addition to the objectives listed for this section, the assessment questions below can help you make your evaluation of the student's success in the six developmental elements. These questions can be used concurrent with the day's exercises and at the end of the 10-day Invitation section.

Does the student demonstrate

- sincere interest and effort to get to know and work cooperatively with all members of the ensemble?
- sensitivity and consideration of the efforts of other group members?
- commitment to the group effort and the task at hand?
- full cooperation in whole-class reflective critiques of the work as it progresses?
- willingness to trust and be trusted? to enable and reassure other members of the ensemble?
- awareness of the immediate environment, including respect for safety and classroom etiquette?
- self-awareness of commitment to assigned tasks?
- personal monitoring of decision making and outcomes?
- focused personal reflection of progress in the developmental elements?
- attention to detail in assigned tasks?
- spontaneity, creativity, and resourcefulness in the application of the developmental elements?
- evidence of learning the developmental elements of theatre and dramatic form as they unfold throughout the exercises?

Rubric

For more formal evaluation, you can use the following rubric. You may wish to reproduce it to share with students when you explain how you will evaluate their early work in this course.

5 **Excellent** The student displays a high level of achievement in all of the developmental elements.

4 **Proficient** The student displays a high level of achievement in the majority of the developmental elements, with moderate achievement in the rest.

3 **Competent** The student displays a moderate level of achievement in all of the developmental elements.

2 **Adequate** The student displays a moderate level of achievement in the majority of the developmental elements, with low achievement in the rest.

1 **Unsatisfactory** The student displays a low level of achievement in all of the developmental elements.

Invitation

Day 1

Safety Introduction (5 minutes)
Distribute copies of BLM 1 and BLM 2 and/or copies of your own classroom safety rules. Have students take them home to read overnight to prepare for discussion the next day.

Everybody Knows My Name (10 minutes)
Have students stand in a circle large enough so that everyone can see everyone else. You may take a place in the circle as well. One at a time in a clockwise direction, have students clap their hands twice and say their names so that everyone can hear. Repeat this at least three times, making sure that everyone is heard and noticed. Now have the students do the same thing again, but this time say the name of the person immediately to the left, having students then say the name of the person immediately to the right. Complicate each round by starting with a different student and by having students say the name of the person two or three spaces to the right or left. Complete the exercise by having one student clap, then point to and name a student across the circle. That student then does the same for another student, who then repeats the action for a third student, and so on until everyone has been named. Have the class congratulate themselves with general applause.

Trust Walk (10 minutes)
In pairs, have students decide who is A and who is B. A closes his or her eyes. B places a hand on A's shoulder and leads A around the room having A touch various objects. A has to describe what he or she is touching. It's a good idea to review the trust and safety rules orally before you begin this exercise. After five minutes have A and B change roles.

What I Saw (10 minutes)
Have students sit in their own spaces anywhere in the room. Direct them to look around the room for one minute, observing as much detail as possible—colors, shapes, objects, textures, and so on. Then ask them to close their eyes for one minute and silently recall how many colors they observed in the room. Have them open their eyes and share how many colors they observed and where they observed them. You might ask those who observed the most colors to indicate where they see those colors in the room. Repeat the exercise with shapes, objects, and textures.

Object A to Z (5 minutes)

Have students form a large circle. Ask one student to name any object beginning with *A*—for example, *apple*. Direct the next student to name an object beginning with *B*, the third with *C*, and so on through the alphabet. If there are more than 26 in the class the 27th student begins again with *A*. Keep going as quickly as possible. See how many times through the alphabet your class can go in five minutes.

Now It's a . . . (5 minutes)

Resources: 3 or 4 simple household or classroom objects

Have students form a large circle. Hand one student a simple object, such as a hairbrush. He or she must demonstrate using the object as if it were something entirely different; for example, a microphone. That student then hands the object to the next student, who must demonstrate a new function, and so on around the circle. Do the same for several more objects. Encourage speed and spontaneity.

Evaluation/Feedback (5 minutes)

Inform students of the six developmental elements they will be building upon during the upcoming days—ensemble-building, trust, observation, self-confidence, concentration, and imagination and creativity. Discuss the importance of each in theatre work.

Ask students to consider how much effort and creativity they put into the class. You might also wish to discuss the criteria you will use to assess their work in these first classes (p. 7).

Day 2

Safety and Etiquette (15 minutes)

Spend a few minutes discussing any questions students may have about the safety rules. Now is also the time when you should review your rules for classroom etiquette. You can use the rules included earlier under Student Safety (p. 5) or establish your own rules.

Your Name Is . . . (15 minutes)

Introduce all students by name, having each student stand and be recognized when you call his or her name. (You can take a role in this, if you think it's useful.) Have students then walk around the room meeting each other with a handshake and a greeting that uses the student's name, such as "Hello, Michael." Give students enough time to meet and greet everyone. Now ask students to walk around again and choose a partner they don't know very well, if at all. Have students introduce themselves briefly to their partners, telling a little about themselves. Then have the class sit in a large circle. Ask each student to introduce his or her partner, giving as much information about that person as he or she can remember. Ask: Were they accurate? Did they listen effectively?

Life Map (5 minutes)

Resources: one pencil and one index card per student

Hand out one index card per student. Have them write on one side of the card the three things that they are most proud of in their lives so far. On the other side have them write the three things that they most want to achieve this year. When they are finished, have students share one thing from either side of their cards with the class. At this point you can collect the cards for future reference. Be sure to have students write their names on their cards.

Blind Trust Line (10 minutes)

Have students stand around the room in their own spaces with their eyes closed. Prompt them to think for a few minutes about the heights of their fellow classmates: Who is the tallest? the shortest? With their eyes still closed, have them very carefully form a line from tallest to shortest. Remind them to do this gently, slowly, and as quietly as possible. Don't give too many instructions: let them work out a way to accomplish the task. On completion, have them open their eyes and see how well they did.

Evaluation/Feedback (5 minutes)

Discuss the exercises and their implications for a theatre student. Ask students if they understand the need for safety rules and classroom etiquette. Ask who couldn't resist opening his or her eyes in the Blind Trust Exercise and discuss why and how it affected their participation.

Day 3

Name That Person (15 minutes)

Have students find a space in the room and sit comfortably. Choose one student to stand and describe—without naming—a fellow student. (Ask students to be mindful of classroom etiquette and to respect their classmates.) Tell students, as they grasp who is being described, to keep the name to themselves. When you believe that most of the class can identify the person being described, choose a student to name the person. Repeat the exercise involving as many students as possible in describing, being described, or identifying the subject.

Raising the Subject of Trust (15 minutes)

Split the class into groups of eight students. Only one group should work at any one time; the other groups should observe from a safe distance. With one group only, have a student—the subject—lie on the floor with arms crossed over his or her chest. Position three students on either side of the subject and one at the head. Explain to the students that the objective is to raise the subject to a standing position. The subject should not resist and may need to stiffen his or her body somewhat to facilitate the exercise. The student at the head and the three students on either side raise the upper body and legs of the subject.

Change the subject in the group and repeat. Do this until all or most group members have had a turn at being the subject. Rotate groups and subjects until everyone has had a turn at being the subject and at being part of a group raising the subject.

Memory Tray (10 minutes)

Resources: a tray full of many small assorted items—at least twice as many as there are students in class—plus a cloth to cover the tray and items

In advance, prepare a tray full of small objects: a pencil, a paper clip, a key, a coin, and so on; anything that may be close to hand in the average office or classroom. Have students sit in as tight a circle as possible. Place the tray in the middle of the circle and let students observe it for one minute. Cover the tray with a cloth. Then have students, one at a time, identify one object that was on the tray, without repeating any object. When a student fails to identify an object he or she stands. The game continues until the last student is sitting or all the objects have been identified. (You may find it useful to prepare a checklist of items for your own reference.)

Group Object Story (5 minutes)
Resources: tray of objects used in Memory Tray
Ask students to sit in a tight circle. Place the tray of objects in the center of the circle. Explain that you will select one object, at random, from the tray. You will then begin a story with one sentence only, after which you will hand the item to a student who will develop the story with one further sentence. At any time any student can change the object by selecting another from the tray. The idea, however, is to continue a plausible story. You can stop the story at any time by taking the object from the last student and finding a sentence that ends the story plausibly or by asking that student to do so.

Evaluation/Feedback (5 minutes)
Discuss the exercises of the day with questions such as the following:

- In what ways were you imaginative or creative in the exercises while keeping within the established rules?

- In what ways are you increasing your powers of observation?

- How do you believe these exercises might be valuable for the people working in acting, directing, producing, and technical theatre, as well as in other careers?

- Do you all know each other by now?

- In what ways do you feel we are building a cooperative group—an ensemble?

- In what ways do you feel we are building trust?

Day 4

Who Am I Now? (15 minutes)
Resources: index cards prepared with names
Have the class sit in a large semicircle. Give everyone an index card. Place two chairs facing the students. Ask for two volunteers to sit in the chairs. Quietly, without letting the class know, give the volunteers the name—written on an index card—of a well-known character such as a movie star, a politician, or a school personality. Ask one volunteer to act as the character, the other as an interviewer. The interviewer asks the character 20 questions about himself or herself. The character must answer as briefly as possible, preferably with yes or no. The rest of the class must decide

who the character is and write the name secretly on their index cards. When the 20 questions are done, let students tell whose names they have written. Repeat the exercise several times.

Blindfold Touch (10 minutes)
Resources: a blindfold
(NOTE: Blindfold work is very difficult for many students. Early blindfold exercises are best done simply with eyes closed. This exercise is a gentle progression. It isolates the blindfolded person for safety. Don't be tempted to use several blindfolded subjects at one time.)

Have the students stand in a large circle. Select a volunteer and have that student stand in the middle of the circle. Blindfold him or her. Tell the volunteer to stand still while you gently place your hand on his or her shoulder. Ask the rest of the class to change places in the circle very quietly. Then steer the blindfolded student very gently to someone in the circle. Place the blindfolded person's hand gently on the face of the person in the circle. Have the blindfolded person gently touch the face and try to figure out who it might be, without telling yet. Gently steer the blindfolded student back to the center and ask the others to change places quietly once more. Take off the blindfold and ask the volunteer whom he or she touched. Repeat with other volunteers.

Blindfold Observation (5 minutes)
Resources: a blindfold
Have the students stand in a large circle. Blindfold a volunteer in the center. Have the students in the circle trade places very quietly. Then, silently, lead one student from the circle to a place (outside the classroom if necessary) where he or she can't be seen. Take the blindfold off the volunteer and ask who is missing. Have the missing person return. Repeat with other volunteers.

Sculptured Emotions (5 minutes)
Split the class into five groups. Give each group an emotion—verbally or written on an index card. Have each group plan and form a sculpture with their bodies that displays the emotion. Show these sculptures one by one to the other groups and have them identify the emotion.

A Reason for Everything (10 minutes)
Have students form a large circle. Describe the following progression to the students: One person makes a statement, such as "The room was hot." A second person responds with a reason, "Because someone left the door open." A third person describes an action or result that logically progresses from the previous statement and reason, "So Robert asked Philip to close the door." A fourth person gives a reason, "Because Philip was standing next to it." A fifth person makes a further observation, "But then the air conditioner kicked in, making it too cold," and a sixth might add a reason, "Because there's never a happy medium in Arizona!"

The exercise can progress in several ways. You might have students add statements, reasons, and results in random order, progressing one-by-one around the circle, or you might select students by pointing or touching them gently on the shoulder. Stop when a sequence of actions or ideas reaches a logical conclusion or gets too silly. Start again with another opening statement.

Evaluation/Feedback (5 minutes)

Ask students to evaluate their involvement in the exercises of the day. How involved were they in each one? Could they have tried harder? What do they think they have learned from these exercises? Remind them of the six developmental elements (which you may wish to copy on the chalkboard) and invite students to comment on how they are building in these areas.

Day 5

Fizz-Buzz (10 minutes)

Have students form a circle, preferably standing. Ask students to count off around the circle. Starting at a different point, have them count off again, substituting "fizz" for the number 5 and any multiple of 5. You may need to try this several times before everyone gets the hang of it. Then switch to 7 and multiples of 7, substituting "buzz." Next attempt to go around the circle with the students counting off, doing the substitutions for both multiples of 5 and of 7 ("1, 2, 3, 4, fizz, 6, buzz, 8, 9, fizz, 11, 12, 13, buzz, fizz, 16, 17, 18, 19, fizz, buzz, 22, 23, 24, fizz," and so on) until you make it to 35—which is "fizz-buzz." You might add a layer of complexity by reversing the direction round the circle after each *fizz* and *buzz*. Try to get the group to complete the whole fizz-buzz without error in under 10 minutes. Explain to students that Fizz-Buzz isn't intended to test their math skills but is used as a vocal warm-up and concentration exercise.

Yeah, Let's! (5 minutes)

Set up some rules before beginning the game: No suggestions of violence. No leaving the room. No actions that would violate any school rules or classroom etiquette. (You may wish to add other rules of your own.)

Begin the game by suggesting an action, such as "Let's touch all four walls." Everyone in class replies, "Yeah, Let's!" and proceeds to do it. As this is being accomplished, someone else calls out a new suggestion, such as "Let's all hop on our right legs." Everyone replies, "Yeah, Let's!," and does so. Someone else might then suggest, "Let's all lie down on the floor and close our eyes," or "Let's all clap our hands three times," and so on until everyone is warmed up.

Word Chains (5 minutes)

Form a large circle. Begin the exercise by having a student say the first word that enters his or her mind, such as "snow." The second student repeats "snow" and adds a word associated with it, such as "white." The third student repeats "white" and adds a further associated word, such as "cloud." Have students keep going in this way, gradually building speed.

Proverb Pictures (25 minutes)

Resources: index cards with written proverbs

Split the class into five groups. Give each group a proverb written on an index card; for example, "Blood is thicker than water" or "Better late than never." Give each group some space to work in. Ask them to discuss the proverb and to think of a simple story that might lead to a character saying the proverb as a way of understanding or explaining what happens. Then have them construct three frozen pictures or sculptures—one each for the beginning, middle, and end of the story. Tell them to find a smooth way of moving from the first to the second to the third picture/sculpture. Then ask them to select a narrator who will tell the story as it unfolds through the movements. The narrator might end by saying the proverb—or the whole group might recite it in unison. Have the groups perform one by one for the whole class.

Evaluation/Feedback (5 minutes)

Because this is likely to be the last class for the first week of the course, you may wish to discuss the progress students have made so far and explain expectations for next week. You might make BLMs 139, 140 Student Self-Assessment available for students to self-assess their progress thus far.

Day 6

Name Ball (3 minutes)

Resources: soccer ball, football, or volleyball

Have students form a large circle. Place a ball in the center. Run to the center of the circle, pick up the ball, and call the name of a student aloud as you pass the ball to him or her. This first student runs to the center with the ball and places it on the floor, calling another student's name. The second student goes to the center while the first student takes his or her place in the circle. The second student picks up the ball and calls a third student's name, and so on. Try to involve the entire class.

Trippingly on the Tongue (7 minutes)

Have students form a large circle. Take a place in the circle and speak a line you have memorized from Shakespeare (or any other playwright). Hamlet's speech from act III, scene ii of *Hamlet* is a good choice: "Speak the speech, I pray you, as I pronounced it to you, trippingly on the tongue." Speak it as if you were performing the role. Have the students, in unison, attempt to copy your phrasing. Then begin to play with the line. Teach it to the students in phrases: "Speak the speech . . . I pray you . . . as I pronounced it to you . . . trippingly on the tongue." With these phrases, have students speed up, slow down, declaim loudly, speak gently and thoughtfully, experiment with different rhythms, and generally have fun playing with the words. Then put the whole line back together. To end the exercise, have each student recite the line in his or her own way.

Tricky Inquisitor Dialogue (10 minutes)

Have students sit in a circle. Ask for a volunteer to play the Inquisitor. He or she moves around inside the circle, stops, looks directly at one particular student, and asks a question about anything—current affairs, music, school news, and so on. The student addressed must not answer; the answer must be given by the student on the right. Repeat with variations of having students one, two, or three places to the right or left give the answers. Students making a mistake must leave the circle. (Laughing while the Inquisitor looks directly at you is considered a mistake.) Continue until too few people are left. Switch Inquisitors and have several more inquisitions. Remind students who are out that they must remain quiet and attentive to the game.

Body Adverbs (25 minutes)

Resources: tape or CD player with assorted music recordings; prepared list of adverbs

Have students find a space in the room where they can move freely. Ask them to create three different body positions, such as lying down, sitting, standing, crouching, stretching, balancing, and so on. When they have three positions each, have them find a way of moving smoothly from position one to position two to position three. Each student now has a short movement sequence. Ask students to demonstrate their sequences to the class.

Then have students form groups of three and teach each other their sequences. Each group then finds an effective way of linking the nine positions together in one sequence, working quickly and spontaneously without thinking too much. (Be flexible: allow students to add or drop elements creatively.) When they are ready, give each group an adverb, for example, *agonizingly, exuberantly, harshly, lovingly,* and so on, with which they will color their movement sequence. Play selected music while students practice their nine-part movement pieces with their adverbs. Have each group perform their Body Adverb for the class.

Evaluation/Feedback (5 minutes)

In these exercises students should have been aware of language and movement, speech and rhythm, imagination and creativity, and the effectiveness of group work. Discuss these elements with them. Ask how self-confident students felt when acting as the Inquisitor or when answering questions. Ask how effective and creative they felt working individually and in groups on the Body Adverbs. Ask how they felt about speaking the line aloud.

Day 7

Vocal A to Z (3 minutes)

Have students form a large circle. Lead them through vocalizing the alphabet using vocal variation. Use different rhythms by varying the number of letters in a phrase; for example: *abc . . . cde . . . efg . . . h . . . i . . . jjjjjjjjj . . . klmnop . . . q . . . r . . .* and so on.

Elongate some letters, shorten others, vary the pitch up to very high and down to very low, change the tempo from fast to slow. Have students repeat each phrase in unison.

Vocal Vibrations (3 minutes)

Have students form a circle. Lead them through examples of nose, throat, and chest vocal resonators. (Don't use the term *resonator*, which is explained in Chapter 1; simply talk about the vibrating quality of their voices.) Ask them to make *nnnnnnnnn* sounds to feel the sound vibrating in their noses; to make *mmmmmmmmm* sounds to feel their lips vibrating; to make *eeeeeeeee* sounds to feel their mouth cavities vibrate. Lead them from *ooooooooo* sounds to *oo-oo-oo-oo-oo-oo* sounds for throat vibration and from *uuuuuuuuu* sounds to *aaaaaaaaa* sounds for chest vibration. Ask them to speculate why a voice with strong vibrations might be important for work onstage.

My Own Voice (4 minutes)

Have students find a space in the room and relax. Have them flop over from the waist like rag dolls, relaxing and breathing freely (knees should be bent and the head should hang loose). Then have them slowly inhale as they roll up and rise to a comfortable upright position. When their lungs are full, have them use their stored air to make an *aaaaaaaaa* sound continuously until all their breath is gone, and then flop over into the rag doll again. They should relax and breathe for a few moments before inhaling slowly as they rise and repeat the sound. Repeat this several times until the students appear to be completely loosened up.

You may wish to explain at this point that an uninhibited voice will produce the most natural sound. If students are able to free themselves completely, the resulting sounds will be at their natural pitches. It's important that students of theatre find their natural voices as early as possible in their training.

Volleyball! (5 minutes)

Split the class into four teams: A, B, C, and D. Have teams A and B pantomime a volleyball game for 2 minutes while teams C and D watch. Students on the spectator teams get to decide who wins the match. Then have teams C and D play for 2 minutes while teams A and B watch. Finally have a 1-minute play-off for the winning teams.

(Students are engaged in pantomime during this exercise. *Pantomime* is defined in the student text on page 28. You may use this term if you like or wait to use it and define it for students when they reach that page in the student text.)

Up-and-Down Trust (10 minutes)

Split the class into groups of eight. Remind students how they raised each other in the Raising the Subject of Trust exercise (see Day 3). Proceed as in that exercise with three people on either side of the subject and one at his or her head. This time students raise the subject to standing position and then lower him or her back to the ground. (Remember to let only one group at a time proceed with the exercise. Make sure you have complete control throughout. Stand very close, so that you can offer physical support if needed.)

Character and Self (20 minutes)

Have the students form pairs. Give the pairs a little time (5 minutes) to practice for a one-minute scene in which each student will play one of his or her parents or guardians in a parent-teacher conference with you. You can play yourself or another teacher. The conference will be about the student. After the preparation time, play out these brief scenes one at a time.

Evaluation/Feedback (5 minutes)

Discuss the goals of the class, student participation and effort, and the effectiveness of the exercises. Were they believable? Were students aware of revealing themselves while playing another character? Did they throw themselves whole-heartedly into the exercises?

Day 8

The Bomb (10 minutes)

Resources: drawing of a bomb; a damp cloth; assorted classroom objects (chairs, bags, jackets, anything bulky)

Before students enter the classroom, place a drawing of a bomb somewhere in the room. Hide the bomb by placing other objects over it in a natural manner. Place the damp cloth somewhere in plain sight.

When the students enter the room, give them the following instructions:

- You must remain silent; you may only communicate without words.

- A bomb has been placed somewhere in the room. You must find it and disarm it by covering it with a damp cloth.

- If there is any noise, or if anything slips or falls while you are moving it, the bomb will explode!

You might put these instructions on the chalkboard in advance and point to them silently when students enter. Or, to add suspense, you might meet students outside the room and hand them printed instructions. If carried out successfully, the drama will begin and end in silence.

Raising Trust to New Heights (10 minutes)

Split the class into groups of eight. Remind students how they raised each other in the Up-and-Down-Trust exercise (see Day 7). Proceed as in that exercise with three people on either side of the subject and one at his or her head. This time students lift the subject from the floor to chest height and lower him or her to the floor again.

Tell students that their complete concentration is necessary throughout. Tell them also to avoid the temptation to lift higher. Remember to let only one group at a time proceed with the exercise. Ensure that the students are calm and quiet before and during this exercise, and make sure you have complete control throughout.

Stand very close, so that you can offer physical support if needed. If any students feel insecure, do not force them to participate.

Character Readings (25 minutes)

Resources: assorted newspaper or magazine articles
(NOTE: You may want to have students prepare for this activity in advance—perhaps as a homework assignment—by selecting their character and newspaper or magazine article on a subject that you have approved.)

Have students select an article to read (one that takes 60–90 seconds should be sufficient). Ask each student to select a well-known public figure, such as a movie star or a politician and read the article out loud as that character would do. (If students have prepared in advance, they may wish to add a simple costume element, such as a hat or scarf, to aid their characterizations.)

Evaluation/Feedback (5 minutes)

Ask students to share their experiences in performing the characters during the Character Readings exercise. Was Character Readings more real, more believable than The Bomb? If so, why? How do they feel about trust in this class so far?

Day 9

Handshake (5 minutes)

Have students form groups of three. Have two of them meet and shake hands. The third student tells the first two when to freeze their image in a still picture. The third student then decides who they are and what they are doing—business people making a deal, friends meeting or parting, someone accepting a new job, and so on. At the third student's signal, the first two immediately unfreeze their image and begin a dialogue as the characters designated. Have students change places so that everyone gets a chance at deciding one scene and playing in one or two.

(Students are engaged in improvisation during this exercise. *Improvisation* is defined in the student text on page 36. You may use this term if you like or wait to use it and define it for students when they reach that page in the student text.)

Passing Shapes (5 minutes)

Have students stand in two lines on either side of the room, backs to the wall. The first student decides on an object that he or she picks up (in pantomime) from the floor, carries across the room, and hands to the first person in the line opposite. Tell students to think about the real object and to try to demonstrate the size and weight of the object through hand position and muscle tension. The student who received the object carries it across the room and hands it to the second student in line, and so on, until the last student receives the object. This student then carries it back to the first person and tells what he or she thinks the object is. Repeat as time allows.

(Students are engaged in pantomime during this exercise. *Pantomime* is defined in the student text on page 28. You may use this term if you like or wait to use it and define it for students when they reach that page in the student text.)

Character Description (5 minutes)

Place three chairs in a straight line on one side of the classroom or on the stage or a raised platform if you have one. Have three student volunteers sit in the chairs. Together they decide on a given character—real (such as a famous politician, a movie star, or a musician) or imaginary (such as a popular cartoon character or a character from a well-known story). The rest of the class asks questions of the three students to find out the name of the character. The three students answer each question in a complete sentence, but each speaks only one word in the sentence at a time. The completion of the sentence can be indicated by a drop in the voice or some other more obvious signal. Tell audience members to raise their hands when they think they know the name of the character. (Only one suggestion per audience member is allowed.) Play the game several times.

(Students are engaged in improvisation during this exercise. *Improvisation* is defined in the student text on page 36. You may use this term if you like or wait to use it and define it for students when they reach that page in the student text.)

Movement Works (20 minutes)

Resources: tape or CD player with assorted music recordings

Have students find their own spaces in the room. Tell them to choose a simple action—such as making a cup of instant coffee, brushing their teeth, or washing a car—and to work out a realistic portrayal of that action. Direct them to do this silently, without words or sound effects.

When these actions are developed, tell students to exaggerate their movements—to imagine, for example, that the car wash bucket and sponge have become extra large, the cup and spoon enormous, the toothbrush gargantuan.

Ask students to do the whole thing from beginning to end but to repeat particular sections of the movement that they enjoy, or that seem interesting from a creative point of view.

Now ask them to concentrate solely on these more interesting movements. Ask them to experiment with their movements, to make them mechanical or animal-like, or to exaggerate them even further, allowing their bodies to move smoothly from one position to another and back again, repeating sections that seem enjoyable. Ask students to select a sequence of these movements that they can repeat with some clarity and accuracy.

Next, have students form groups of three and teach each other their action sequences. Have the groups devise a way of combining the collective patterns that they have created into a group choreography.

Finally, have the groups perform their collective Movement Works for the class while you play music that you have selected.

Evaluation/Feedback (5 minutes)

Tell students that the goal of the exercises in this class period was to extend the range of their creativity through physical and verbal improvisation. Ask students how they feel they met this goal.

Day 10

Voice and Body Mirrors (5 minutes)

Have students pair up and then separate to stand on opposite sides of the room. Each student will work with his or her partner across the room. One side is A, the other is B. A begins with quiet, subtle sounds that B must copy exactly. B then adds movement that A must copy exactly. Tell students to try to make their movement and sound exchanges so smooth that someone new coming into the room would not be sure of who is leading who. A and B then exchange roles. Finally, let students switch leadership of sound or movement as they see fit, going back and forth without having to stop, giving and taking naturally. Stop the exercise and have the class watch particularly interesting examples of pair work.

Sound Scenes (5 minutes)

Have students find their own spaces. Tell them they will use no words in this exercise, but they should add verbal sound effects.

Ask them to imagine having in their hands the controls of a radio-controlled airplane. Let them fly their planes for about 15 seconds. Now tell students that the models are war planes—fighters and bombers. They attack each other, and some of the planes crash. After a short time, call all the surviving planes back to land. Next, tell students to pretend to move across a very marshy, boggy piece of land. At every step they must pull their boots out of the oozing mud.

Finally, tell students to act as though they are surveying the ground for a housing development and to start building the houses—measuring and sawing wood, hammering nails, pouring concrete, and so on.

(Students are engaged in pantomime during this exercise. *Pantomime* is defined in the student text on page 28. You may use this term if you like or wait to use it and define it for students when they reach that page in the student text.)

Movement by Design (25–30 minutes)

Resources: samples of interesting geometric designs (such as on fabric swatches, wallpaper samples, and in magazines) that include a variety of colors and geometric shapes

(NOTE: You may want to have students prepare for this activity in advance—perhaps as a homework assignment—by finding design samples with strong geometric and color design elements.)

Divide the class into groups of six or seven. Give them a few minutes to study the design samples in their group and note the dominant colors and basic geometric shapes in the designs. Ask them to discuss whether the shapes and colors have any universal significance (for example, a yellow circle might signify the sun). Next have each group choose one or more of their designs to recreate with their bodies. Ask them to try and evoke the color and mood of the designs, as well as any particular significance each holds. Encourage them to try to make the geometric shapes move in patterns. For example, they might have a curving line move around a square. They can also develop design sequences, moving from one design to another, altering the speed and rhythm of the changes.

If the design doesn't call for the whole group, suggest that one or two students refer to the design samples and help coordinate the other group members' positions and movements from a perspective outside the design.

For the last five minutes of the exercise, talk about how shapes and colors might figure in creating onstage pictures. What shapes look interesting together? Which colors and designs evoke emotional response? What are those responses—excitement? security? tension? comfort?

(As an alternative to working from existing design samples, you might have each group create their own original geometric design with markers on paper, utilizing various shapes and colors.)

Evaluation/Feedback (10 minutes)
Allow a slightly longer time period for feedback at the end of this day's lesson. Ask students to think about and to evaluate themselves in the areas of the six developmental elements that have been addressed over the past 10 days. To these, add recognizing theatre as a performing art and as a medium for learning and pleasure. Ask students to evaluate themselves, the class as a whole, and themselves *as* members of the whole. Begin with discussions. Then ask students to write their evaluations and return them the following day. Collect these so that you can have an idea of each student's self-assessment. Make copies for your files as future reference and give the originals back to students after they are introduced to the Theatre Notebook in the student text (p. xx). Encourage them at that time to add their evaluation comments in their Theatre Notebooks.

Exploration Lessons

Chapter 1

Acting

E X P L O R A T I O N

THE LANGUAGE OF THEATRE

articulation

articulators

gesture

improvise

inflection

pantomime

project

resonance

resonators

script

Overview

This chapter prompts students to engage in self-awareness to prepare for creating characters both similar to and different from
themselves; introduces the concept of the body and voice as the
actor's primary instrument and the need to explore and train that
instrument; defines and illustrates pantomime and its uses onstage;
introduces improvisation and its importance in theatre, especially
for developing story and characters; and describes storytelling as a
precursor of acting and as a modern craft with transferable skills to
both theatre and nontheatre careers.

Students participate in a range of basic movement and vocal
exercises, as well as pantomime, improvisation, and storytelling
exercises and activities. Group work allows students to explore an
important component of theatre: the ensemble ethic.

Objectives

- The student will begin to develop self-awareness through
  observation and partner feedback.
- The student will be able to understand and execute physical
  warm-ups to develop relaxation, body coordination, and
  flexibility.
- The student will be able to use pantomime techniques to create the illusion of concrete objects and to create a story with a
  beginning, a middle, and an end.
- The student will be able to understand and execute vocal
  warm-ups to develop breath control, range, and flexibility, as
  well as to expand his or her ability to interpret dramatic literature vocally.
- The student will be able to understand and use improvisational
  skills for character creation and exploration, storyline development, and spontaneity.
- The student will understand the historical, social, cultural, and
  creative aspects of storytelling.
- The student will be able to use and define appropriate theatre
  vocabulary, including vocal production and interpretation,
  pantomime, and improvisation.
- The student will demonstrate an understanding of journaling
  with regards to acting exercises and creative development.

Resources

- Large open space; nonconcrete flooring; at least 2 square feet per student
- Tape player; taped music of two types: 1) upbeat, with steady beat, and 2) soothing and relaxing
- BLM 2 Movement Safety
- BLM 103 Chapter 1 Test: Acting
- BLM 123 Section 1 Answer Key
- BLM 127 Alternative Assessment Rubric: Project 1
- BLMs 139, 140 Student Self-Assessment
- OVH 15 Visual Arts Link: Chapter 1 Acting

> There are many additional resources included in the *Teacher's Resource Book*. For those that relate to this chapter, see the chart at the front of this *Teacher's Manual* (pp. xviii–xxi).

Customizing

At-Risk Students

Focus on the exercises that enhance practical life skills, such as improvisation (problem solving through role playing) and story-telling (communication skills).

Classrooms with Limited Resources

A classroom (with furniture moved well out of the way) or a gym will suffice for exercises and activities requiring a large space.

Students with Physical Disabilities

Identify the physical exercises that students are capable of performing. Break down these exercises into smaller sections and allow a longer period of time, giving more individual attention to students who need it.

Cooperative Learning

Have students first work in small groups to master one of the physical exercises and then lead the class in learning that exercise. Suggest that individuals share exercises with the class to add to warm-up routines. Encourage students to give each other constructive feedback.

Visual Arts Link

Using OVH 15, with *The Luncheon of the Boating Party* by Pierre-Auguste Renoir, ask students to imagine that they are one of the people in the painting who is telling the story of that day to his or her grandchildren 50 years later. They can write their stories or simply plan them out and tell them to the rest of the class. Point out to students that by telling their stories rather than reading them, they provide themselves with possibilities for improvisation.

Side-Coaching Tips

The following are ideas to help provide ongoing support as students do exercises and activities:

Improving Body Image

Encourage students to become comfortable with their own bodies—no matter the size or shape—and to respect themselves as they prepare their bodies for performance. Stress that performance does not require a perfect body but one that is a healthy, functioning tool for self-expression.

Dressing for Exercise

Students should wear loose-fitting clothing that permits freedom of movement. Tight-fitting and overly baggy clothing impede movement; the latter also prevents observation of possible movement or breathing problems, or excessive muscle tension.

Using Music

Appropriate music will facilitate exercises. Upbeat music is helpful for keeping movements steady and consistent. Soft, relaxing music (or silence) will facilitate cool-down exercises.

Ensuring Proper Technique

Throughout the exercises, movements should be fluid, never jerky. Monitor students during breathing exercises; proper diaphragmatic breathing causes in-and-out movement of the abdomen and chest, not up-and-down movement of the shoulders. When students tip their heads backward, watch that they do not drop them back and compress the vertebrae in their necks but stretch up with their chins. (You might want to review with students the guidelines listed in BLM 2.)

Avoiding Strain

Warn students not to force any movement. Remind them to breathe deeply, which brings necessary oxygen to working muscles, keeps the body relaxed, and aids concentration.

Balancing a Workout

Any exercise that stretches or works one side of the body should be balanced with equal work on the opposite side.

Vocalizing

There are many different ways of vocalizing. Encourage students to experiment with pitch, volume, tempo, phrasing, and quality.

Caring for the Voice

Caring for the voice entails keeping one's head and neck warm, avoiding smoke-filled air, getting enough sleep, limiting vocal strain, and avoiding milk and milk products before performances.

Handling Stage Fright

To alleviate students' stage fright, have students first work in groups rather than individually. Give them plenty of time to rehearse pantomimes and storytelling. For the improvisations, remind students that there are no mistakes in improvisation since every action and statement is an opportunity to advance the story.

Giving Everyone a Chance

Make sure everyone is involved and no one is "standing in the wings." Subdivide groups that are too large and impose time limits on performances to keep things moving and to promote fresh character assignments.

Support for Activities

The activities may be used as in-class activities, homework assignments, or as opportunities for extra-credit work. Most can be completed in one or two days.

Encourage students to put their own spin on the performance activities, especially the situation improvisations and pantomimes. The only requirements should be that the performance tell a story with a beginning, middle, and end and follow the conventions of the form, be it pantomime, improvisation, or storytelling.

Student Assessment

Assessment may be accomplished by measuring achievement of the objectives outlined at the beginning of this lesson plan. Students may demonstrate their success at meeting those objectives through participation in class exercises and class discussion and fulfillment of assigned activities. You may wish to create your own rubric for assessment. See pages xxii–xxvi for guidance on creating rubrics. A chapter test (BLM 103) may also be used. Project 1: Telling a Story may be used as an alternative, performance-based assessment. (BLM 127 provides a rubric for assessing student performance on this project.)

Self- and group-assessment may take the form of journaling entries in the students' Theatre Notebooks, some of which are part of the chapter exercises and activities. Other entries could address self-assessment questions (BLMs 139, 140). Finally, students might also reflect upon any constructive feedback they have received from their peers.

The Storytelling Tradition

E X P L O R A T I O N

Overview

This historical profile introduces the storytelling tradition, which some historians include among the origins of theatre. The profile discusses the purposes that storytelling serves, the connection between oral and written literary traditions, the role of the West African storyteller/historian known as a griot, the performance aspects of the griot's job, and the overall importance of the oral tradition. The profile concludes with an excerpt from a West African tale, *Sundiata, an Epic of Old Mali*, that students may use to practice the griot's art themselves. The Try It Out and Extension activities emphasize acting.

Objectives

- The student will demonstrate an understanding of the historical and cultural significance of storytelling and the role of the griot.
- The student will understand the importance of and can demonstrate a variety of vocal characterizations and interpretations through the art of storytelling.
- The student will be able to understand and apply basic dramatic timing and pacing techniques, which are utilized to enhance the dramatic tension in storytelling.
- The student will be able to demonstrate the use of language and sounds to express mood, feeling, and emotion.

Resources

- A number of small drums and other percussion instruments
- Space sufficient for the storyteller to stand and move and for students to react and participate
- An Outline of Theatre History (student text, pp. 1–15)
- BLM 115 Historical Profile Test: The Storytelling Tradition

- BLM 123 Section 1 Answer Key
- BLMs 139, 140 Student Self-Assessment
- BLMs 141, 142 Research Activities: The Storytelling Tradition

> There are many additional resources included in the *Teacher's Resource Book*. For those that relate to this historical profile, see the chart at the front of this *Teacher's Manual* (pp. xviii–xxi).

Customizing

English-Language Learners

Have students tell the story in their own language; they should clearly communicate the story's intent through gestures and inflection. The storyteller may also teach the audience a repeated phrase to which they will respond with a short, rhythmic phrase in the language being used.

Links to Literature/Language Arts

Have students read and discuss the portion of *Roots* in which Alex Haley describes his encounter with a West African griot who recited Haley's family history.

Research

Have students who would like to know more about the storytelling tradition do one of the research activities on BLMs 141 and 142.

Side-Coaching Tips

The excerpt, *Sundiata, an Epic of Old Mali* includes sidenotes—comments and questions—in the margins. The suggestions that follow also provide ongoing support as students practice storytelling:

Using Chanting and Rhythm

For a chanted response, choose a short rhythmic phrase like "Hero Sundiata." Students may experiment with various ways of saying the phrase to hear different rhythmic patterns and natural inflections. Remind students in the audience that their response and the percussion accompaniment must serve and reflect the story, not overpower it.

Using Different Voices

Encourage students to create distinct vocal characterizations by imitating in their speech animal or environmental sounds, such as a shrieking hawk or a thundering waterfall.

Alternative Activities

The following activities may be used as in-class or homework assignments or as opportunities for extra-credit work:

Retelling an Urban Legend

Have students relate in their Theatre Notebooks an urban legend, such as the one about the albino alligators living in the sewers of New York City. Students could then prepare an oral retelling of the story, complete with sound effects and movement.

Relating an Ethnic Story

Have students retell a folktale that is representative of their heritage. After each story, encourage students to ask the storyteller questions so that they understand the customs and traditions of that particular culture.

Student Assessment

Assessment may be accomplished by measuring achievement of the objectives outlined at the beginning of this lesson plan. Students may demonstrate their success at meeting those objectives through participation in class discussions and in their interpretation of the excerpt from the story, *Sundiata, an Epic of Old Mali*. They may also complete the profile test on BLM 115. You may wish to create your own rubric for assessment. See pages xxii–xxvi for guidance on creating rubrics.

Self-assessment may take the form of journaling entries in the students' Theatre Notebooks. Other entries could address self-assessment questions (BLMs 139, 140). Finally, students might also reflect upon any constructive feedback they have received from their peers.

Chapter 2

Directing & Producing

E X P L O R A T I O N

Overview

In this chapter, students begin to learn about theatre production by examining issues such as who is ultimately responsible for making decisions, what is involved in planning and financing the production of a play, and how to attract an audience. The leadership roles of director and producer are introduced, including their responsibilities, skills, and staffs. The members of the production team are also identified, and the initial process of developing a production concept within a budget is described. Finally, students become familiar with the theatre itself: the proscenium, thrust, and arena stages are discussed; the theatre building layout is detailed; and the stage areas are identified. The activities reinforce the concepts introduced with experiential learning opportunities.

THE LANGUAGE OF THEATRE

apron
arena stage
downstage
house
production concept
proscenium stage
scenery
stage manager
thrust stage
upstage (noun)

Objectives

- The student will be able to understand the general roles of the director and the stage manager in a theatre production.
- The student will be able to understand the general role of the producer in a theatre production.
- The student will be able to identify the standard stage spaces (for example, proscenium and thrust).
- The student will be able to use and define appropriate theatre vocabulary including terms describing stage areas, backstage areas, and front-of-house locations.
- The student will be able to analyze the theatre spaces and equipment available for production planning.
- The student will understand the roles and responsibilities of the business and front-of-house staff.

Resources

- Access to a stage or performance area
- BLM 6 Job Shadow Agreement
- BLM 37 Stage Areas
- BLM 104 Chapter 2 Test: Directing & Producing

- BLM 123 Section 1 Answer Key
- BLM 128 Alternative Assessment Rubric: Project 6
- BLMs 139, 140 Student Self-Assessment
- OVH 5 Theatre Space Layout
- OVH 16 Visual Arts Link: Chapter 2 Directing & Producing

> There are many additional resources included in the *Teacher's Resource Book*. For those that relate to this chapter, see the chart at the front of this *Teacher's Manual* (pp. xviii–xxi).

Customizing

Creative Challenge

Encourage directing students to reflect in their Theatre Notebooks on the performance space used in the last play they saw. They should identify the possible reasons the director chose that particular play to stage in that theatre space.

Links to Literature/Language Arts

Emphasize the play reading and elementary analysis aspects of theatre production. As students read different plays, encourage them to note the various periods and themes. Students can either write in their Theatre Notebooks or discuss in class their impressions of the plays' suitability for production.

Students with Physical Disabilities

Have students examine local theatre spaces to see if they are accessible to populations with special needs. If not accessible, have students suggest ways that the theatres might be improved.

Visual Arts Link

Using OVH 16, with *The Great Wave of Kanagawa* by Katsushika Hokusai, have students imagine this painting is a backdrop for a set. Have them discuss the type of performance space a backdrop like this would require to fulfill its dramatic impact in expressing the power and size of a tidal wave. What kind of production concept would they develop for a play in which this backdrop was a part of the set? Have students write their ideas in their Theatre Notebooks.

Side-Coaching Tips

The following are ideas to help provide ongoing support as students do activities:

Experiential Learning

Be on the lookout for opportunities to give students a feel for the experience of directing and producing a play. Job shadowing, listening to or conducting an interview with a professional, inviting a local director to visit with the class, attending a performance, or touring a theatre are all activities that would help students recognize the effort and cooperation involved in directing and producing.

Exploring Your School's Facilities

Discuss with students the value of researching past productions and analyzing their school's theatre space and inventory. (You might use BLM 37 and OVH 5 to prepare students for examining their school's theatre space.) Questions to consider could include what they might learn or gain by doing so. You might, for example, explain how taking inventory will give students a sense of collective ownership.

Developing Interests

Encourage students to explore all aspects of theatre production without limiting or classifying themselves. For example, some students may sign up for the course because they want to act but may later discover that they are more interested in producing or directing. Students should use their Theatre Notebooks to record personal observations, ideas, and discoveries; to save playbills; to make lists of plays they want to read and see; and to preserve design samples and concepts.

Support for Activities

The activities may be used as in-class activities, homework assignments, field trip options, or as opportunities for extra-credit work. The first two, Form a Play Club and Job Shadow—Business Manager, may continue through the year or semester. (Be sure to review with students the guidelines for job shadowing on BLM 6.) The others can be completed in two days to one week.

Student Assessment

Assessment may be accomplished by measuring achievement of the objectives outlined at the beginning of this lesson plan. Students may demonstrate their success at meeting those objectives through participation in class discussion and fulfillment of assigned activities. You may wish to create your own rubric for assessment. See pages xxii–xxvi for guidance on creating rubrics. A chapter test (BLM 104) may also be used. Project 6: Analyzing Theatre Spaces may be used as an alternative, performance-based assessment. (BLM 128 provides a rubric for assessing student performance on this project.)

Self- and group-assessment may take the form of journaling entries in the students' Theatre Notebooks, some of which are part of the chapter activities. Others entries could address self-assessment questions (BLMs 139, 140). Finally, students might also reflect upon any constructive feedback they have received from their peers.

Historical Profile

Sophocles

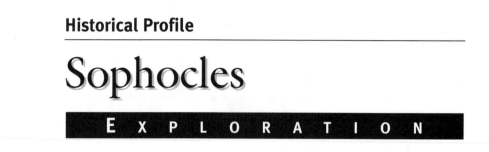

E X P L O R A T I O N

Overview

This historical profile introduces students to the theatre traditions of ancient Greece and, in particular, to the work of the playwright Sophocles. The profile describes the open-air theatre space where dramas were staged; presents the conventions of Greek drama; discusses the costumes and masks worn by Greek actors; and concludes with a scene from Sophocles' tragedy *Antigone*. Students are encouraged to make masks for the scene and to stage it in a large space, such as a gymnasium, to develop a deeper appreciation of the Greek theatre tradition and its influence on modern theatre. The Try It Out and Extension activities emphasize directing.

Objectives

- The student will be able to describe the relationship between Greek drama and Greek religious practices.
- The student will be able to describe the physical appearance and structure of a theatre space in ancient Greece.
- The student will be able to identify Sophocles, his representative plays, and his influence on the growth of theatre.

Resources

- Space suitable for a scene with two actors: if possible, a space large enough to create the effect of an open-air theatre
- Art supplies, including cardboard, for making masks
- Two robes or draping fabric for costumes
- An Outline of Theatre History (student text, pp. 1–15)
- BLM 116 Historical Profile Test: Sophocles
- BLM 123 Section 1 Answer Key
- BLMs 139, 140 Student Self-Assessment
- BLMs 143, 144 Research Activities: Greek Theatre

There are many additional resources included in the *Teacher's Resource Book*. For those that relate to this historical profile, see the chart at the front of this *Teacher's Manual* (pp. xviii–xxi).

Customizing

At-Risk Students
Read the scene from *Antigone* aloud and have students vote on whether they would side with Antigone or Ismene in this conflict. Identify the main issues that surface in the scene, and discuss how they might be resolved and whether they have any modern parallels.

Creative Challenge
Have directing students stage the scene in the school gymnasium or football field. They will need to identify the difficulties posed by such large, open performance spaces and devise appropriate solutions for an effective performance.

Research
Have students who would like to know more about Greek theatre do one of the research activities on BLMs 143 and 144.

Side-Coaching Tips

The scene from *Antigone* includes sidenotes—comments and questions—in the margins. The suggestions that follow also provide ongoing support as students direct or perform the scene:

Using Masks
Remind students that performing with a full-face mask means that their body language and tone of voice are especially important because they cannot rely on facial expressions to convey their emotions. Have students practice both projecting different tones of voice through their masks and using simple movements to express their characters' feelings and attitudes.

Portraying Emotions
Encourage directing students to identify with their actors the strong emotions in this scene. Before having their actors practice reciting their lines, they should first concentrate on each emotion individually until the actors can effectively portray it through movement and voice.

Alternative Activities

The following activities may be used as in-class or homework assignments or as opportunities for extra-credit work:

Writing Diary Entries
Have students write diary entries for Antigone and Ismene that express each character's feelings immediately before and after the scene.

Staging an Adaptation
Have students stage the scene between Antigone and Ismene from Jean Anouilh's modern version of *Antigone*.

Student Assessment

Assessment may be accomplished by measuring achievement of the objectives outlined at the beginning of this lesson plan. Students may demonstrate their success at meeting those objectives through participation in class discussions and in their role in the performance of the scene from *Antigone*. They may also complete the profile test on BLM 116. You may wish to create your own rubric for assessment. See pages xxii–xxvi for guidance on creating rubrics.

Self-assessment may take the form of journaling entries in the students' Theatre Notebooks. Other entries could address self-assessment questions (BLMs 139, 140). Finally, students might also reflect upon any constructive feedback they have received from their peers.

Chapter 3

Technical Theatre

E X P L O R A T I O N

Overview

This chapter identifies the stage crew—the artistic and technical people responsible for creating the overall look and sound of a performance and for running a live production. The stage crew encompasses six technical areas: set construction, props, lighting, sound, costumes, and makeup. The functions of each crew and its leader are detailed, and each crew is provided with lists of recommended equipment and supplies; basic skills to master in each area; and specific safety rules. Students can learn and practice skills in each area by doing the activities at the end of the chapter.

Objectives

- The student will be able to identify and discuss the responsibilities, safety regulations, and duties of the various technical crews.

- The student will be able to demonstrate an understanding and working knowledge of the basic techniques, equipment, supplies, and safety requirements for theatrical scenic design, construction, and operation.

- The student will be able to demonstrate an understanding and working knowledge of the basic techniques, equipment, fixtures, supplies, electricity, and safety requirements for theatrical lighting and sound design, construction, and operation.

- The student will be able to demonstrate an understanding and working knowledge of the basic techniques, equipment, supplies, and safety requirements for theatrical costume design, construction, and care.

- The student will be able to demonstrate an understanding and working knowledge of the basic techniques, equipment, supplies, and safety requirements for theatrical makeup design, application, and removal.

- The student will be able to explain the qualities that make theatre a collaborative art and demonstrate discipline in artistic endeavors by working on projects and productions with others.

- The student will be able to use and define appropriate theatre vocabulary.

THE LANGUAGE OF THEATRE

batten
cue
drop or **backdrop**
flat
platform
property or **prop**
set
stage crew
throw

Resources

- Shop space, tools, and construction supplies as detailed in chapter
- Lighting system, instruments, and supplies as detailed in chapter
- Sound system, recording equipment, and supplies as detailed in chapter
- Costume shop, tools, and supplies as detailed in chapter
- Makeup supplies and facilities as detailed in chapter
- BLM 6 Job Shadow Agreement
- BLM 58 Scene Shop Safety Activity
- BLM 60 Electricity Safety Activity
- BLM 62 Costume and Makeup Safety Activity
- BLM 105 Chapter 3 Test: Technical Theatre
- BLM 123 Section 1 Answer Key
- BLM 129 Alternative Assessment Rubric: Project 10
- BLMs 139, 140 Student Self-Assessment
- OVH 17 Visual Arts Link: Chapter 3 Technical Theatre

> There are many additional resources included in the *Teacher's Resource Book*. For those that relate to this chapter, see the chart at the front of this *Teacher's Manual* (pp. xviii–xxi).

Customizing

Classrooms with Limited Resources

If there is a limited scene shop or none at all, ask for cooperation from the Art, Home Economics, and Industrial Arts departments. They may be willing to share their facilities or at least allow students to tour them to gather ideas for establishing their own facilities.

Cooperative Learning

Have the class divide into small groups. Each group will be responsible for creating a finished product in one technical area. Each group will share their learning experience and finished product with the rest of the class.

English-Language Learners

Make sure that safety rules are understood by all. If necessary, translate the rules and then post them. Visually demonstrate the techniques for using equipment so that students will learn by imitation.

Visual Arts Link

Using OVH 17, with *Pink Room* by A. Schevtshenko, have students imagine that this is a set rendering for an upcoming production. In small groups, they can discuss and make a list of the basic equipment for scenic design that they might use to build this set. Have groups present and explain their ideas to the other groups.

Side-Coaching Tips

The following are ideas to help provide ongoing support as students do activities:

Safety Safety Safety

Students are learning to operate potentially dangerous equipment. Emphasize that safety regulations must be strictly observed at all times. Protective clothing and gear must always be used, and safety practices must always be followed. Stress that carelessness can result in serious injury or even death. (As a way of encouraging students to think about issues of technical theatre safety, you may want students to do the activities on BLMs 58, 60, and 62.)

Visual Demonstration and Hands-on Practice

To help solidify students' learning of this chapter, it's a good idea to demonstrate for them the proper use of the tools, skills, and processes discussed. It's also helpful for students to physically handle the various tools in order to identify them and their purposes.

Varying Skills and Interests

Few students will be skilled in all areas of technical theatre. Encourage students to explore each area. Some may discover they have certain skills, talents, or interests of which they were previously unaware.

Support for Activities

The activities may be used as in-class activities, homework assignments, or as opportunities for extra-credit work. Students can utilize the activities to begin honing a skill they find intriguing. They can work as individuals, in pairs, or in small groups. Remind students that you must be present whenever they are working with any kind of power tool. Encourage them to be creative in their work, for example, in their music or fabric choices. When applying straight, as opposed to character, makeup, students should try to achieve a look that appears natural when viewed onstage. The Job Shadow—Makeup Artist activity may continue through the semester or year. (Be sure to review with students the guidelines for job shadowing on BLM 6.)

Student Assessment

Assessment may be accomplished by measuring achievement of the objectives outlined at the beginning of this lesson plan. Students may demonstrate their success at meeting those objectives through participation in class discussion and fulfillment of assigned activities. You may wish to create your own rubric for assessment. See pages xxii–xxvi for guidance on creating rubrics. A chapter test (BLM 105) may also be used. Project 10: Makeup Scrapbook may be used as an alternative, performance-based assessment. (BLM 129 provides a rubric for assessing student performance on this project.)

Self- and group-assessment may take the form of journaling entries in the students' Theatre Notebooks, some of which are part of the chapter activities. Other entries could address self-assessment questions (BLMs 139, 140). Finally, students might also reflect upon any constructive feedback they have received from their peers.

Project 1

Telling a Story

E X P L O R A T I O N

Assignment

In a small group, perform a story using movement and narration.

Objectives

- The student will be able to use language and literature for developing communication skills, personal exploration, and social interaction.
- The student will be able to demonstrate body coordination and flexibility using movement for creative self-expression.

Resources

- Performance space, such as a classroom or school theatre
- Anthologies of short stories, fables, and/or fairy tales
- BLM 13 Storytelling Guidelines
- BLM 14 Storytelling Ideas
- BLM 127 Alternative Assessment Rubric: Project 1
- BLMs 139, 140 Student Self-Assessment

> There are many additional resources included in the *Teacher's Resource Book*. For those that relate to this project, see the chart at the front of this *Teacher's Manual* (pp. xviii–xxi).

Creating

If students are having difficulty selecting or developing a story, you might have them look at BLMs 13 and 14. Encourage them to simplify their narratives if the storyline becomes unwieldy.

Performing

Remind students that the pantomime and the spoken narrative should not compete for the audience's attention but should blend together.

Responding

You and the students may assess the projects using a rubric you have created. (See pages xxii–xxvi for guidance in creating rubrics.) Remind students to give each other positive, constructive feedback. Students may also use the prompts on BLMs 139, 140 to do self-assessment. Students may record their reactions to their own and to others' projects in their Theatre Notebooks. This project, which is an alternative assessment for Chapter 1, may also be evaluated by using BLM 127.

Project 2

Animal Pantomime

EXPLORATION

Assignment

Create a pantomime story based on the exploration of animal movement.

Objectives

- The student will be able to demonstrate the ability to create a pantomime story, using pantomime techniques for objects, environment, and character.
- The student will be able to explore a variety of characters from life in imagined situations while developing observation skills.

Resources

- Performance space, such as a classroom or school theatre
- Reference material on animal behavior; for example, *National Geographic, National Wildlife,* and other nature magazines; encyclopedias and other reference works on wildlife, in text or multimedia form; wildlife videos
- BLMs 139, 140 Student Self-Assessment

There are many additional resources included in the *Teacher's Resource Book*. For those that relate to this project, see the chart at the front of this *Teacher's Manual* (pp. xviii–xxi).

Creating

As students develop their stories and actions, help them identify visual elements that will contribute to telling the story. Suggest a performance time frame so that the pantomimes are neither too elaborate nor too brief.

Performing

Students must maintain clear and distinct actions. If using music or background sounds, the students need to make sure the tape is cued and that it contributes to the story and coordinates with the actions of the story.

Responding

You and the students may assess the projects using a rubric you have created. (See pages xxii–xxvi for guidance in creating rubrics.) Remind students to give each other positive, constructive feedback. Students may also use the prompts on BLMs 139, 140 to do self-assessment. Students may record their reactions to their own and to others' projects in their Theatre Notebooks.

Project 3

Improvisation and Tableau

EXPLORATION

Assignment

In a small group, create a tableau to represent a picture and develop an improvisation based on the situation depicted in the picture.

Objectives

- The student will be able to utilize physical elements by creating and selecting movement qualities for a specific character.
- The student will be able to portray a character and establish simple relationships with other characters.

Resources

- Performance space, such as a classroom, school theatre, or mirrored dance studio
- References such as art books, magazines, newspapers, and family picture albums
- Polaroid camera and film (optional)
- BLM 11 Improvisation Guidelines
- BLMs 139, 140 Student Self-Assessment

There are many additional resources included in the *Teacher's Resource Book*. For those that relate to this project, see the chart at the front of this *Teacher's Manual* (pp. xviii–xxi).

Creating

If your class is focusing on a particular period in theatre history, students could choose works of art from that era. You might have them review the improvisation guidelines on BLM 11.

Performing

Students need a number of rehearsals to develop a sense of confidence in themselves as a group. A group that works well together facilitates the individual's ability to initiate or respond to action naturally and in character during performance. Agreeing on and rehearsing a prearranged signal for ending is very important.

Responding

You and the students may assess the projects using a rubric you have created. (See pages xxii–xxvi for guidance in creating rubrics.) Remind students to give each other positive, constructive feedback. Students may also use the prompts on BLMs 139, 140 to do self-assessment. Students may record their reactions to their own and to others' projects in their Theatre Notebooks.

Project 4

Soundscapes

E X P L O R A T I O N

Assignment

Work with a partner or small group to create a performance combining movement with sound.

Objectives

- The student will be able to utilize language and sounds to express mood, feeling, and emotion.
- The student will be able to use listening skills to develop a greater awareness of an environment.

Resources

- Performance space, such as a classroom or school theatre
- Tape recorder (methods 1 and 5)
- Commercial sound effects tape or CD (method 5)
- Audiotape splicing equipment and materials as detailed in chapter (methods 1, 3, and 5)
- Various percussion instruments or sound-making objects (method 3)
- BLM 63 Sound Basics
- BLMs 139, 140 Student Self-Assessment

There are many additional resources included in the *Teacher's Resource Book*. For those that relate to this project, see the chart at the front of this *Teacher's Manual* (pp. xviii–xxi).

Creating

Don't shortcut the individual listening, visualizing, imagining, and writing part of the process. This provides the basis for the creativity in the project. Partners or groups should consider and try to incorporate the input and ideas of everyone involved. You might want students to review the guidelines in BLM 63.

Performing

Coordinating the movements and sounds will take practice, so students need to remember to allow time for rehearsal. Groups may either divide up and assign technical and performance responsibilities amongst themselves or involve all group members in both providing sounds and performing the movements.

Responding

You and the students may assess the projects using a rubric you have created. (See pages xxii–xxvi for guidance in creating rubrics.) Remind students to give each other positive, constructive feedback. Students may also use the prompts on BLMs 139, 140 to do self-assessment. Students may record their reactions to their own and to others' projects in their Theatre Notebooks.

Project 5

Perspectives on Theatre Spaces

EXPLORATION

Assignment

Work with a group of four actors to explore theatre spaces from an audience's point of view and document your conclusions.

Objectives

- The student will understand how different types of stages (thrust, arena, proscenium) affect directing and audience perception.
- The student will understand how different stage areas (upstage, downstage, and so on) affect audience interpretation and perception.

Resources

- Open area in which students can work
- Masking tape

- BLM 37 Stage Areas
- BLMs 139, 140 Student Self-Assessment

> There are many additional resources included in the *Teacher's Resource Book*. For those that relate to this project, see the chart at the front of this *Teacher's Manual* (pp. xviii–xxi).

Creating

You might provide students with BLM 37 as a reference. The student observer can shorten the drawing time if 20 blank perspective diagrams are prepared in advance by making copies of a hand-drawn original.

Presenting

When students redraw or tidy up their sketches, it may be helpful to use a different color of ink or marker to identify each actor. If students verbally present their findings, they shouldn't read their notes but refer to them and speak spontaneously.

Responding

You and the students may assess the projects using a rubric you have created. (See pages xxii–xxvi for guidance in creating rubrics.) Remind students to give each other positive, constructive feedback. Students may also use the prompts on BLMs 139, 140 to do self-assessment. Students may record their reactions to their own and to others' projects in their Theatre Notebooks.

Project 6

Analyzing Theatre Spaces

E X P L O R A T I O N

Assignment

Present an illustrated analysis of various kinds of area theatre spaces.

Objectives

- The student will be able to apply research skills in production planning.
- The student will be able to demonstrate an understanding of basic and alternative theatre spaces.

Resources

- Permission to visit and photograph various theatre spaces at school and in the community
- Video camera, Polaroid camera, 35mm camera, sketch pad
- TV/VCR, photo album, scrapbook, or poster board for classroom presentation
- BLM 128 Alternative Assessment Rubric: Project 6
- BLMs 139, 140 Student Self-Assessment

> There are many additional resources included in the *Teacher's Resource Book*. For those that relate to this project, see the chart at the front of this *Teacher's Manual* (pp. xviii–xxi).

Creating

If theatre spaces in the area are plentiful, encourage students to try to include a thrust stage, an arena stage, and a nontraditional performance space. Students should take good notes or keep a log of their images in order to clearly identify their videotape or pictures at a later time. Remind students to leave the space exactly as they found it, especially if they move an object to get a shot of something.

Presenting

Students should know their material. They need to be prepared to answer questions and support their opinions or observations.

Responding

You and the students may assess the projects using a rubric you have created. (See pages xxii–xxvi for guidance in creating rubrics.) Remind students to give each other positive, constructive feedback. Students may also use the prompts on BLMs 139, 140 to do self-assessment. Students may record their reactions to their own and to others' projects in their Theatre Notebooks. This project, which is an alternative assessment for Chapter 2, may also be evaluated by using BLM 128.

Building a Model Stage

EXPLORATION

Assignment

Using cardboard or another lightweight material, build a scale model of your school's theatre space.

Objectives

- The student will be able to use an understanding of measurement and scale to draw a rendering and build a model of a theatre.

- The student will be able to demonstrate a working knowledge of the types of stages, the stage components (fly space, apron, wings, and so forth), and how each stage type and component affects the functions of the technical elements.

Resources

- Access to scene shop and its tools
- Cardboard, balsa, or foamcore
- Poster board
- Various supplies such as glue, tape, paint, and fabric
- Appropriate safety equipment
- BLM 57 Scene Shop Safety Tips
- BLMs 139, 140 Student Self-Assessment

There are many additional resources included in the *Teacher's Resource Book*. For those that relate to this project, see the chart at the front of this *Teacher's Manual* (pp. xviii–xxi).

Creating

Double-check all measurements and record them accurately. Students should observe safety rules throughout the process. You might have them review the tips on BLM 57.

Presenting

Since the models will be somewhat fragile, students should be sure to display them on a steady, sturdy surface. If they plan to utilize their models when planning future productions, they should store them carefully in a safe place.

Responding

You and the students may assess the project using a rubric you have created. (See pages xxii–xxvi for guidance in creating rubrics.) Remind students to give each other positive, constructive feedback. Students may also use the prompts on BLMs 139, 140 to do self-assessment. Students may record their reactions to their own and to others' projects in their Theatre Notebooks. This project may also be evaluated by using the sample rubric provided on page xxiv.

Project 8

Shop Inventory

E X P L O R A T I O N

Assignment

Inventory the equipment and supplies in the workspaces of a technical area: set construction and props, costumes, or lighting.

Objectives

- The student will be able to identify and understand the function of the tools, equipment, and supplies used in the technical areas of theatre.
- The student will be able to apply organization skills in the setup and maintenance of technical areas of theatre.

Resources

- Access to technical theatre areas
- BLMs 139, 140 Student Self-Assessment

There are many additional resources included in the *Teacher's Resource Book*. For those that relate to this project, see the chart at the front of this *Teacher's Manual* (pp. xviii–xxi).

Creating

Students should definitely plan a strategy before charging into work areas. Before they begin, have students create an appropriate form to record their inventory. They may use the sample on page 119 of the student book or create their own. It would also be best to do the inventory when the technical areas are relatively quiet.

Presenting

If the inventories are posted, it would be valuable to be able to make additions, deletions, or changes to keep the inventory current. It may also be useful to keep the inventory records on a computer so that information can be more easily updated. Suggest that students schedule periodic updates and designate responsibilities for updating. This will help ensure that the inventory stays current and therefore usable.

Responding

You and the students may assess the projects using a rubric you have created. (See pages xxii–xxvi for guidance in creating rubrics.) Remind students to give each other positive, constructive feedback. Students may also use the prompts on BLMs 139, 140 to do self-assessment. Students may record their reactions to their own and to others' projects in their Theatre Notebooks.

Project 9

Sewing Demonstration Board

E X P L O R A T I O N

Assignment

Practice and present basic seams and research their uses.

Objectives

- The student will understand the basics of costume construction.
- The student will be able to apply and develop basic presentation skills.

Resources

- Access to costume shop and its tools
- Cotton or cotton/polyester blend fabric scraps
- Thread
- Poster board, cardboard, foamcore, or bulletin board
- Fabric marking pen or labels
- Double-sided basting tape or glue stick
- BLMs 139, 140 Student Self-Assessment

> There are many additional resources included in the *Teacher's Resource Book*. For those that relate to this project, see the chart at the front of this *Teacher's Manual* (pp. xviii–xxi).

Creating

For longer-lasting, better-looking samples, encourage students to use pinking shears to cut their fabric pieces. Students should use thread that contrasts and shows up clearly against the fabric so that the stitching may be seen clearly.

Presenting

As they work, students should record their opinions on seam use and types of fabric so that they may share their impressions with the class. Students may also teach other students the skills they have learned.

Responding

You and the students may assess the projects using a rubric you have created. (See pages xxii–xxvi for guidance in creating rubrics.) Remind students to give each other positive, constructive feedback. Students may also use the prompts on BLMs 139, 140 to do self-assessment. Students may record their reactions to their own and to others' projects in their Theatre Notebooks.

Makeup Scrapbook

E X P L O R A T I O N

Assignment

Create a scrapbook showing a variety of facial types and hairstyles and organize them according to a system.

Objectives

• The student will be able to apply research skills to explore the history of costumes, hairstyles, and makeup.

• The student will be able to demonstrate basic organizational and presentation skills.

Resources

• References such as family portraits, books, magazines, newspapers, catalogs, and multimedia resources such as CD-ROMs and the Internet

• Three-ring binder, scrapbook, or photo album

• BLM 129 Alternative Assessment Rubric: Project 10

• BLMs 139, 140 Student Self-Assessment

> There are many additional resources included in the *Teacher's Resource Book*. For those that relate to this project, see the chart at the front of this *Teacher's Manual* (pp. xviii–xxi).

Creating

Creating a table of contents may help students organize their collection. Students may also wish to collect photos of makeup techniques for depicting animal faces, fantasy looks, or inanimate objects. To experiment with various colors or haircuts on a sketch or photo, students could create the alterations as drawings on an overlay of clear plastic or acetate paper.

Presenting

Students should be encouraged to use their collections as a basis to practice makeup and hairstyles. Students could also pick up used wigs at garage sales to practice on (after shampooing them). When students have perfected a "look," they could model it for the class.

Responding

You and the students may assess the projects using a rubric you have created. (See pages xxii–xxvi for guidance in creating rubrics.) Remind students to give each other positive, constructive feedback. Students may also use the prompts on BLMs 139, 140 to do self-assessment. Students may record their reactions to their own and to others' projects in their Theatre Notebooks. This project, which is an alternative assessment for Chapter 3, may also be evaluated by using BLM 129.

Preparation
Lessons

Chapter 4

Acting

PREPARATION

THE LANGUAGE OF THEATRE

beats

cold reading

cross

focus

master gesture

open

shared position

subtext

upstage (verb)

Overview

Having explored basic acting techniques in Chapter 1, students can now prepare for particular dramatic roles. This chapter describes how the characterization process draws upon an actor's observations, experiences, and imagination. It also discusses character motivation and behavior and shows how elements such as a character's background, style of movement, voice, motivation and behavior, and subtext are developed in order to create a believable character. The basics of stage movement and audition preparation are also covered.

The exercises and activities guide students in building three-dimensional characters and in understanding audition techniques and etiquette.

Objectives

- The student will explore and develop sensory and observation skills to heighten awareness of self, others, and their environment.

- The student will understand and be able to execute the basics of stage movement.

- The student will be able to demonstrate the use of analysis skills when creating characters by developing physical, emotional, and social dimensions of characters that are culturally and historically true to the text.

- The student will be able to create believable characters and actions through the use of their sensory equipment.

- The student will be able to identify and execute professional auditioning and rehearsal techniques and etiquette.

- The student will be able to demonstrate an understanding of the biographical and motivational aspects of building a character.

- The student will be able to develop and utilize memorization techniques for performance, as well as demonstrate an understanding of cold reading techniques for rehearsal and auditioning.

- The student will be able to use and define appropriate theatre vocabulary including *objective, subtext, obstacle,* and *fourth wall.*

Resources

- Performance space that works as both a proscenium and an arena stage
- Scenery flats with doors
- Straight chairs and tables
- Mirrors, possibly on makeup tables
- Tape recorders
- 3 x 5 cards
- Costume and hand props
- Videocamera (if available)
- *The Book of Scenes for Aspiring Actors* (or other books of scenes)
- *The Book of Monologues for Aspiring Actors* (or other books of monologues)
- BLM 106 Chapter 4 Test: Acting
- BLM 124 Section 2 Answer Key
- BLM 130 Alternative Assessment Rubric: Project 12
- BLMs 139, 140 Student Self-Assessment
- OVH 18 Visual Arts Link: Chapter 4 Acting

> There are many additional resources included in the *Teacher's Resource Book*. For those that relate to this chapter, see the chart at the front of this *Teacher's Manual* (pp. xviii–xxi).

Customizing

At-Risk Students

Students from high-risk environments may have cultivated self-protective personas that cannot be easily put aside. Work on establishing a sense of trust among your students that will allow them to take risks in expressing a range of emotions and attitudes. You might, for example, ask them to submit to you certain entries from their Theatre Notebooks, or you could provide a box in which students could put suggestions or ideas they have. Always be sure to give feedback in such instances.

Creative Challenge

Students who are talented in some ways—for example, in analyzing subtext—can be challenged in others, such as in stage movement. Pair students with strengths in different areas and encourage them to share their knowledge and skills with each other.

English-Language Learners

Allow English-language learners to work freely, using their own language in some of the exercises. Encourage bilingual students to translate for the class.

Visual Arts Link

Using OVH 18, with *Dominique y Veronica* by Bernardita Zegers, have students discuss the kind of characters they might create based on the images of the man and woman in this painting. If they need direction, tell them to start by developing a background for these people (see pages 136–137 of the student text). They should also consider how the characters might move. What is his or her leading center? Can they think of a master gesture for each of these characters? When presenting, students should become their characters and provide the background information about their character, incorporating movement in the presentation. Others in the class can determine the character's leading center and master gesture.

Side-Coaching Tips

The following are ideas to help provide ongoing support as students do exercises and activities:

Taking Notes

After characterization exercises, students should record their observations in their Theatre Notebooks. Encourage students to share their thoughts during class discussions, or collect the Theatre Notebooks and provide each student with written feedback.

Discovering Motivation

Emphasize that understanding motivation and behavior is a life-long study, one that draws on experiences such as reading and people watching.

Discerning Background

Point out that two people observing a third may legitimately disagree on that person's background. For example, two people observing a man dining in a restaurant may disagree on his social status. One person may say that the man is poor based on his shabby clothes. The other person may observe his impeccable table manners as proof of his social background or status. Have students share experiences in which they disagreed with someone else on the background of a person or in which they were surprised to discover certain things about a person's background. They can improvise scenes based on their discussions and on the consequences of accurately or inaccurately discerning background.

Studying a Script

Stress that analyzing and building a character is not merely an exercise of the imagination but is rooted in a play's stage directions and dialogue. The director's concept must also be considered.

Moving on Stage

Build in time during class for students to practice basic stage movements and to improve their posture and poise.

Using Silence

Stress the importance of listening and reacting to one another's lines and actions. Discuss as a class how pauses in dialogue can communicate volumes of information to the audience. For example, students might recall a situation in which their parents' silence communicated anger, such as the time they came home two hours late. Suggest that students incorporate pauses in appropriate places during their improvisation and monologues and then write about the effect of the pauses on pacing and meaning of the scenes in their Theatre Notebooks.

Relying on External Factors

Warn students not to rely too much on external factors, such as costumes or props. Although they can inspire and reinforce characterization, they are not a substitute for it.

Support for Activities

The activities may be used as in-class activities, homework assignments, or as opportunities for extra-credit work. Most can be completed in one or two days.

Encourage students to incorporate the pantomime, improvisation, and storytelling skills covered in Chapter 1 as they experiment with characterization. Emphasize that building a character is a physical, emotional, and intellectual process, one involving constant analysis and experimentation.

Student Assessment

Assessment may be accomplished by measuring achievement of the objectives outlined at the beginning of this lesson plan. Students may demonstrate their success at meeting those objectives through participation in the exercises and class discussion and fulfillment of assigned activities. You may wish to create your own rubric for assessment. See pages xxii–xxvi for guidance on creating rubrics. A chapter test (BLM 106) may also be used. Project 12: Building Characters may be used as an alternative, performance-based assessment. (BLM 130 provides a rubric for assessing student performance on this project.)

Self- and group-assessment may take the form of journaling entries in the students' Theatre Notebooks, some of which are part of the chapter exercises and activities. Other entries could address self-assessment questions (BLMs 139, 140). Finally, students might also reflect upon any constructive feedback they have received from their peers.

Shakespeare

Overview

This historical profile briefly summarizes Shakespeare's life and accomplishments; describes Elizabethan theatre spaces; and discusses Elizabethan costuming and acting styles. An excerpt from *A Midsummer Night's Dream* allows students to analyze character motivation and to use gesture, movement, and line interpretation in dramatizing a comic scene. The Try It Out and Extension activities emphasize acting.

Objectives

- The student will be able to demonstrate a basic knowledge of the life and works of William Shakespeare.

- The student will be able to identify the structure and significance of the Globe theatre.

- The student will be able to identify and describe appropriate styles of costumes and accessories for characters of Shakespeare's plays if set during the Elizabethan period.

- The student will be able to demonstrate through performance a basic understanding of the use of the language of Shakespeare's plays.

- The student will be able to demonstrate appropriate stage movement in the performance of material from Shakespeare's plays.

Resources

- Space suitable for a scene with four actors and large enough to replicate a thrust stage
- An Outline of Theatre History (student text, pp. 1–15)
- *The Book of Scenes for Aspiring Actors* (or other books of scenes)
- *The Book of Monologues for Aspiring Actors* (or other books of monologues)
- BLM 117 Historical Profile Test: Shakespeare
- BLM 124 Section 2 Answer Key

- BLMs 139, 140 Student Self-Assessment
- BLMs 145, 146 Research Activities: Elizabethan Theatre
- OVH 13 Diagram: The Globe Theatre

There are many additional resources included in the *Teacher's Resource Book*. For those that relate to this historical profile, see the chart at the front of this *Teacher's Manual* (pp. xviii–xxi).

Customizing

English-Language Learners

If language difficulties prevent some students from understanding the scene excerpt, you might group these students with a classmate who does grasp the events and can explain them. Together the students could paraphrase the scene into contemporary English.

Cooperative Learning

After all performances have been given, allow students to self-evaluate within their group. Allow each group to perform the scene again, once all the groups have rehearsed and made changes based on their evaluations. Then lead the class in a discussion, comparing the two performances of each group.

Research

Students who would like to learn more about Elizabethan theatre might do some of the research activities on BLMs 145 and 146.

Visual Learning

Students may be better able to imagine a theatrical performance in Shakespeare's day if they the view the diagram of the Globe Theatre on OVH 13.

Side-Coaching Tips

The scene from *A Midsummer Night's Dream* includes sidenotes—comments and questions—in the margins. The following suggestions also provide ongoing support as students perform the scene:

Differentiating the Characters

If there is not enough contrast between the two female characters or the two male characters, encourage students to make character adjustments. For example, they might distinguish themselves through movement or their manner of vocalizing or costuming.

Waiting for the Laugh

Remind the actors to avoid "stepping" on any laughter that occurs when the men restrain Hermia. Encourage them to wait for the moment when the audience's reaction has peaked and is diminishing.

Alternative Activities

The following activities may be used as in-class or homework assignments or as opportunities for extra-credit work:

Adapting the Scene

Have groups of students perform an adaptation of the scene. Suggest that they adapt the scene to a different time period or culture. Students should consider the new time period or culture when making decisions about characterization, costuming, setting, and so on.

Performing Another Scene

Students could rehearse and perform another scene from one of Shakespeare's plays. (Refer them to *The Book of Scenes for Aspiring Actors*.) In creating their characters, students should go through the characterization process detailed in the text.

Student Assessment

Assessment may be accomplished by measuring achievement of the objectives outlined at the beginning of this lesson plan. Students may demonstrate their success at meeting those objectives through participation in class discussion and in their performance of the scene from *A Midsummer Night's Dream*. They may also complete the profile test on BLM 117. You may wish to create your own rubric for assessment. See pages xxii–xxvi for guidance on creating rubrics.

Self-assessment may take the form of journaling entries in the students' Theatre Notebooks. Other entries could address self-assessment questions (BLMs 139, 140). Finally, students might also reflect upon any constructive feedback they have received from their peers.

Chapter 5

Directing & Producing

PREPARATION

Overview

The chapter begins by presenting the issues faced by directors and producers when choosing a play, and four major genres (comedy, farce, tragedy, and drama) are described. The chapter then explains how a director works with a script by analyzing plot, characters, setting, theme, and style. The director's role in designing a ground plan, planning stage composition, and blocking the actors' movements is discussed, and directions on creating a director's promptbook are provided. The chapter concludes with descriptions of the duties of the producer in handling permissions and publicity and the duties of the stage manager during auditions and rehearsals.

Students engage in a range of activities that develop directing skills such as classifying, choosing, and evaluating a play; analyzing scripts and determining style; and telling stories through stage pictures. Additional activities involve students as producers and include permissions, research, and job shadowing.

Objectives

- The student will be able to understand the history and identify the responsibilities of the director in a theatre production.
- The student will be able to demonstrate an understanding of the elements involved in selecting a play.
- The student will be able to analyze a script by identifying the story elements of a play (plot, character, setting, and theme), plot structure (exposition, inciting incident, rising action, climax, falling action, dénouement), genre (comedy, farce, tragedy, and drama), and style.
- The student will be able to use and define appropriate theatre vocabulary including *staging, protagonist, antagonist,* and *secondary character,* as well as the structural components and elements of a play.
- The student will be able to demonstrate an understanding of focus and stage composition through the use of blocking, lighting, style, body positions, stage areas, levels, and planes.

THE LANGUAGE OF THEATRE

blocking
dénouement
exposition
farce
ground plan
inciting incident
level
plane
royalty
stage (verb)

- The student will be able to understand the role of the director in determining the design concept and style of a production.
- The student will be able to demonstrate the ability to create, develop, and execute the use of a ground plan and promptbook.
- The student will be able to understand the role and responsibilities of the dramaturg.

Resources

- Large open spaces, in classroom or elsewhere
- Chairs, tables, and platforms (if available)
- *The Book of Scenes for Aspiring Actors* (or other books of scenes)
- *The Book of Monologues for Aspiring Actors* (or other books of monologues)
- BLM 6 Job Shadow Agreement
- BLM 107 Chapter 5 Test: Directing & Producing
- BLM 124 Section 2 Answer Key
- BLM 131 Alternative Assessment Rubric: Project 15
- BLMs 139, 140 Student Self-Assessment
- OVH 19 Visual Arts Link: Chapter 5 Directing & Producing

> There are many additional resources included in the *Teacher's Resource Book*. For those that relate to this chapter, see the chart at the front of this *Teacher's Manual* (pp. xviii–xxi).

Customizing

Classrooms with Limited Resources
For directing exercises or activities, relocate to the auditorium, a gym, or a quiet hallway. This will give student directors sufficient space in which to work.

Students with Physical Disabilities
Within safety guidelines, allow and encourage students with disabilities to participate in the activities as best they can. Encourage directing students to brainstorm creative ways to block scenes involving actors who use wheelchairs or other types of equipment.

Links to Literature/Language Arts
Have students work with a partner to select two songs whose lyrics each describe a character. Each pair of students should then develop a brief scene involving both characters. Have students play the two songs and then perform the scene for the class.

Visual Arts Link

Using OVH 19, with *Tower of Eagle: Month of January* (artist unknown), have students imagine this painting as a stage composition. As partners or in small groups, have them analyze the body positions, stage areas, levels, and planes to create focus for this stage composition. Ask them to identify what they think is the focus of the composition. Have them discuss whether any special emphasis (for example, diversified or secondary emphasis) is in effect. Then have each group present their information to the class and discuss their ideas.

Side-Coaching Tips

Rejecting a Script

Review with students the lists of sets, props, and costume demands in a variety of scripts, so that they will better understand how some plays may be too complex for their theatre or budget.

Discussing Genre

Alert students to the various genres of drama by categorizing familiar TV shows and current films.

Identifying the Climax

Applying the questions in the text, analyze with your students a script to determine the play's turning points. Identify which turning point marks the peak of emotional intensity.

Discerning Theme

There are numerous resources students can use to help them discern the theme of particular plays. Encourage them to explore written interviews with playwrights, directors, and actors; reviews of past productions; scholarly studies; topical chat rooms on the Internet; and e-mail with working artists.

Defining Style

To help students understand the term *style*, show short scenes from a variety of films made during the past 60 years and note style elements peculiar to the different time periods.

Composing Stage Pictures

Student directors need to see and participate in a variety of stage pictures. You may want to spend more than one class period having students arrange and rearrange themselves onstage for a number of different scenes. Discuss the emotional or symbolic effects of alternate types of blocking for a scene.

Doing Business

To give students insight into the business aspects of theatre, have students design a plan for raising the money needed to produce a play. This plan could include an ad-selling campaign, a letter requesting funds from local businesses or foundations, or researching available grants.

Support for Activities

The activities may be used as in-class activities, homework assignments, or as opportunities for extra-credit work. Most can be completed in one or two days. Encourage students to use their Theatre Notebooks to record analyses of play elements and to make notes about style issues.

Student Assessment

Assessment may be accomplished by measuring achievement of the objectives outlined at the beginning of this lesson plan. Students may demonstrate their success at meeting those objectives through participation in class discussion and fulfillment of assigned activities. You may wish to create your own rubric for assessment. See pages xxii–xxvi for guidance on creating rubrics. A chapter test (BLM 107) may also be used. Project 15: Creating Stage Pictures may be used as an alternative, performance-based assessment. (BLM 131 provides a rubric for assessing student performance on this project.)

Self- and group-assessment may take the form of journaling entries in the students' Theatre Notebooks, some of which are part of the chapter activities. Other entries could address self-assessment questions (BLMs 139, 140). Finally, students might also reflect upon positive feedback they have received from their peers.

Molière

P R E P A R A T I O N

Overview

This historical profile summarizes Molière's life and accomplishments; describes a typical theatre space of Molière's day; and discusses period costuming and acting style. The profile concludes with a scene from *Tartuffe*, which students are to stage, focusing on blocking, pacing, and delivering rhymed lines. The Try It Out and Extension activities emphasize directing.

Objectives

- The student will be able to demonstrate a basic knowledge of the life and works of Molière, recognizing him as the major playwright of the neoclassical period, the effect of the political arena, and the social significance of his work.

- The student will be able to identify the structure and conventions of the theatres in Molière's professional life.

- The student will be able to identify and describe appropriate styles of costumes and accessories for characters of Molière's plays if set during the neoclassical period.

- The student will be able to demonstrate an understanding of the acting styles used during the neoclassical period.

- The student will develop stage business and motivated blocking appropriate to character and given circumstances.

Resources

- Space suitable for a scene with three actors
- *The Book of Scenes for Aspiring Actors* (or other books of scenes)
- *The Book of Monologues for Aspiring Actors* (or other books of monologues)
- An Outline of Theatre History (student text, pp. 1–15)
- BLM 118 Historical Profile Test: Molière
- BLM 124 Section 2 Answer Key
- BLMs 139, 140 Student Self-Assessment
- BLM 147, 148 Research Activities: Commedia dell'Arte

There are many additional resources included in the *Teacher's Resource Book*. For those that relate to this historical profile, see the chart at the front of this *Teacher's Manual* (pp. xviii–xxi).

Customizing

At-Risk Students

Have students discuss and decide whether the misunderstanding between Valère and Mariane is a universal problem. Ask them to stage scenes based on current situations that relate to this problem.

Creative Challenge

Encourage students not only to embellish this scene with as many technical elements as possible but also to read the entire play and select another scene to direct and stage. To prepare, students should research period costumes, furniture, customs, politics, and so on.

Research

Students who are interested in learning more about commedia dell'arte might do some of the research activities on BLMs 147 and 148.

Side-Coaching Tips

The scene from *Tartuffe* includes sidenotes—comments and questions—in the margins. The suggestions that follow also provide ongoing support as students direct or perform the scene:

Dressing the Part

Encourage students to rehearse with costumes and props, as such gear will influence their character choices. Suggest that Mariane and Dorine wear long, full skirts and that Valère carry a walking stick.

Creating Pictorial Balance

The neoclassical period valued symmetry in art. Suggest that directing students keep that principle in mind as they block the scene.

Alternative Activities

The following activities may be used as in-class or homework assignments or as opportunities for extra-credit work:

Promoting the Play

Have students work together to create an elaborate publicity campaign for a play of their choosing. Students should explore all the avenues available to them, not limit themselves, for example, to news releases and posters.

Talking in Rhymed Couplets

Have students improvise and perform a scene in which the entire dialogue consists of rhymed couplets. Directing students should work with their actors on the delivery so that the language sounds as much as possible like natural speech.

Performing a Monologue

Interested students could rehearse and perform monologues from Molière's work. Refer to *The Book of Monologues for Aspiring Actors* for scenes from *The Misanthrope* and *The Miser*.

Student Assessment

Assessment may be accomplished by measuring achievement of the objectives outlined at the beginning of this lesson plan. Students may demonstrate their success at meeting those objectives through participation in class discussion and in their role in the performance of the scene from *Tartuffe*. They may also complete the profile test on BLM 118. You may wish to create your own rubric for assessment. See pages xxii–xxvi for guidance on creating rubrics.

Self-assessment may take the form of journaling entries in the students' Theatre Notebooks. Other entries could address self-assessment questions (BLMs 139, 140). Finally, students might also reflect upon any constructive feedback they have received from their peers.

Chapter 6

Technical Theatre

PREPARATION

Overview

This chapter opens with a brief history of modern theatrical design and then discusses the four basic elements of production design. Subsequent sections focus on activities in each of the areas of technical theatre that occur early in the production process: set design and set design plans; set construction; joining, bracing, and stiffening scenery; scene painting; prop design and construction; lighting design; sound design; costume design and production; and makeup design.

Each section details the importance of analyzing the script and gives methods for planning and constructing. Activities give students practice in a wide range of technical skills.

Objectives

- The student will be able to demonstrate an understanding and working knowledge of the basic design processes for scenery, props, costumes, makeup, lighting, and sound—through script analysis and planning, as well as by creating sketches, renderings, models, ground plans, charts, lists, and plots.

- The student will be able to demonstrate an understanding and working knowledge of the basic techniques of sound production.

- The student will be able to demonstrate an understanding of the techniques of safely joining, bracing, stiffening, and hanging scenic units.

- The student will be able to distinguish between set, decorative, and hand props and demonstrate an understanding of the various design, construction, and acquisition methods for each.

- The student will be able to demonstrate an understanding of the basic techniques, preparations, clean-up, and safety requirements for scenic painting.

- The student will be able to demonstrate an understanding of the basic design, use, and safe construction techniques of scenic stock units, such as flats, platforms, and drops.

- The student will be able to use and define appropriate technical theatre vocabulary.

Resources

- Design equipment and supplies for sketches and renderings
- Set and prop construction tools and supplies as detailed in chapter
- Lighting supplies as detailed in chapter
- Sound supplies as detailed in chapter
- Costume supplies as detailed in chapter
- Makeup supplies as detailed in chapter
- BLM 6 Job Shadow Agreement
- BLM 108 Chapter 6 Test: Technical Theatre
- BLM 124 Section 2 Answer Key
- BLM 132 Alternative Assessment Rubric: Project 18
- BLMs 139, 140 Student Self-Assessment
- OVH 20 Visual Arts Link: Chapter 6 Technical Theatre

> There are many additional resources included in the *Teacher's Resource Book*. For those that relate to this chapter, see the chart at the front of this *Teacher's Manual* (pp. xviii–xxi).

Customizing

At-Risk Students

Point out to students that many of the technical skills necessary for play production are also requirements in many jobs in the working world. Encourage students to record each skill they learn in their Theatre Notebooks and identify how each can be of use in real life.

Classrooms with Limited Resources

If you lack a backstage scene shop for demonstration and construction, other options would be a woodworking shop, the stage, or even your classroom.

Cooperative Learning

Stress the importance of teamwork in technical theatre. A second pair of eyes or an extra hand is often needed in set construction. For example, while one student is applying stenciling techniques, another student can stand at a distance to ensure proper placement of the stencil.

Visual Arts Link

Using OVH 20, with *The Starry Night Over the Rhone* by Vincent Van Gogh, have groups of students discuss stage techniques they might use to recreate the look and effect of this painting for the stage. They should consider paint and paint techniques, platforms, drops, and lighting that will create mood. One student in each group can act as recorder to take notes on the group discussion. Have each group present and explain their ideas to the rest of the class.

Side-Coaching Tips

Observing Design

Have students jot down design observations and ideas in their Theatre Notebooks. Stress that there are numerous sources from which students can get inspiration for design, including paintings, photographs, movies, museums, and architecture, as well as their own imaginations.

Learning the Tools

Before students construct scenery, review the differences among the varieties of saws, hammers, and screw drivers, as explained in Chapter 3, so they can choose appropriate tools for a particular task.

Preventing a Fire

Onstage, place lights away from sets, gauze curtains, and any other flammable materials. Remind students that the flameproofing of many theatre fabrics does not preclude fires.

Minding the Shop

Organization is key to a well-run and safe shop. Insist that students put away hand tools in their appropriate places after using them. This will cut down on loss and breakage. You might also wish to devise a sign-out system for all tools.

Stirring the Paint

Some paint pigments sink in water, others float. While painting, students should stir paint frequently with a wooden paddle, never with a paint brush. When painting, students should start at the top of scenery and work downward in order to avoid paint drops on finished work.

"Cheating" on Props

Emphasize to students that stage props used on many stages don't need to be exact or authentic since most audience members are too far away to see details. Lead a discussion on how and why props used for arena staging might differ from those for proscenium staging.

Support for Activities

The activities may be used as in-class activities, homework assignments, or as opportunities for extra-credit work. Most can be completed in one or two days. The Job Shadow—Electrician and Job Shadow—Carpenter activities may continue through the semester or year. (Be sure to review the guidelines for job shadowing on BLM 6.)

Many students may be more interested in acting than in technical theatre. Remind them that they need some knowledge of this area in order to make an effective entrance through a door, to handle a prop deftly, to wear a costume naturally, or to be lighted well.

Encourage students with technical talent to take a leadership role in the various activities suggested; to experiment with techniques outside of class; and to sign up for crew work during productions.

Student Assessment

Assessment may be accomplished by measuring achievement of the objectives outlined at the beginning of this lesson plan. Students may demonstrate their success at meeting those objectives through participation in class discussion and fulfillment of assigned activities. You may create your own rubric for assessment. See pages xxii–xxvi for guidance on creating rubrics. A chapter test (BLM 108) may also be used. Project 18: Designing a Set may be used as an alternative performance-based assessment. (BLM 132 provides a rubric for assessing student performance on this project.)

Self- and group-assessment may take the form of journaling entries in the students' Theatre Notebooks, some of which are part of the chapter activities. Other entries could address self-assessment questions (BLMs 139, 140). Finally, students might also reflect upon any constructive feedback they have received from their peers.

Open Dialogue with Stage Movement

PREPARATION

Assignment

With a partner, improvise, rehearse, and perform an open dialogue scene.

Objectives

- The student will be able to explore character analysis and vocal interpretation skills.
- The student will be able to apply and develop basic playwriting and simple dialogue writing skills.

Resources

- Adequate rehearsal space
- BLM 11 Improvisation Guidelines
- BLMs 139, 140 Student Self-Assessment

> There are many additional resources included in the *Teacher's Resource Book*. For those that relate to this project, see the chart at the front of this *Teacher's Manual* (pp. xviii–xxi).

Creating

Deciding on the objectives, circumstances, setting, and conflict quickly will enable students to focus more time on improvising the dialogue and creating the characters. Remind students that sharing the stage means knowing when and how to keep still, listen, or react. To prepare students for creating and performing their improvisation, you might have them review the guidelines on BLM 11.

Performing

To give students practice in staying open, require each character to move twice during the scene.

Responding

You and the students may assess the projects using a rubric you have created. (See pages xxii–xxvi for guidance in creating rubrics.) Remind students to give each other positive, constructive feedback. Students may also use the prompts on BLMs 139, 140 to do self-assessment. Students may record their reactions to their own and to others' projects in their Theatre Notebooks.

Project 12

Building Characters

PREPARATION

Assignment

Develop three distinct characters and perform them in an original scene.

Objective

- The student will be able to explore a variety of characterizations using appropriate physical and vocal qualities.
- The student will be able to apply and develop basic playwriting through improvisation.

Resources

- Rehearsal and performance space
- Costumes and set or hand props (as needed)
- BLM 130 Alternative Assessment Rubric: Project 12
- BLMs 139, 140 Student Self-Assessment

There are many additional resources included in the *Teacher's Resource Book*. For those that relate to this project, see the chart at the front of this *Teacher's Manual* (pp. xviii–xxi).

Creating

Suggest that rehearsing with friends and asking for their reactions, or recording themselves on videotape will help actors develop movements, gestures, and vocal qualities that differentiate the three characters.

Performing

Emphasize to students that moving from one character to another demands focus and concentration. Note, too, that if the monologue contains humorous lines, students should be prepared to ride the laugh before resuming.

Responding

You and the students may assess the projects using a rubric you have created. (See pages xxii–xxvi for guidance in creating rubrics.) Remind students to give each other positive, constructive feedback. Students may also use the prompts on BLMs 139, 140 to do self-assessment. Students may record their reactions to their own and to others' projects in their Theatre Notebooks. This project, which is an alternative assessment for Chapter 4, may also be evaluated by using BLM 130.

Project 13

Delivering a Monologue

P R E P A R A T I O N

Assignment

Perform a two- to three-minute monologue.

Objectives

- The student will be able to explore and demonstrate effective character analysis skills through performance.
- The student will be able to demonstrate an understanding of basic audition skills.

Resources

- *The Book of Scenes for Aspiring Actors* (or other books of scenes)
- *The Book of Monologues for Aspiring Actors* (or other books of monologues)

- Books of short stories
- BLMs 139, 140 Student Self-Assessment

> There are many additional resources included in the *Teacher's Resource Book*. For those that relate to this project, see the chart at the front of this *Teacher's Manual* (pp. xviii–xxi).

Creating

Advise students to develop their monologues systematically by analyzing the script and character, by developing subtext, by determining basic movements and gestures, and by experimenting with vocal volume and pacing. Encourage them to take notes on each of these aspects of characterization so they can make the best use of good ideas and eliminate those that don't work well.

Performing

Remind students that even well-prepared actors can forget lines, movements, or gestures. At such times, they should maintain composure and continue with the monologue.

Responding

You and the students may assess the projects using a rubric you have created. (See pages xxii–xxvi for guidance in creating rubrics.) Remind students to give each other positive, constructive feedback. Students may also use the prompts on BLMs 139, 140 to do self-assessment. Students may record their reactions to their own and to others' projects in their Theatre Notebooks.

Project 14

Entrances and Exits

PREPARATION

Assignment

Plan and perform a scene portraying a jury entering and exiting a jury room before and after deciding a verdict.

Objectives

- The student will be able to demonstrate an understanding of the basic principles of blocking.
- The student will be able to demonstrate an understanding of utilizing entrances and exits for full characterization, as well as for maintaining and creating a complete reality on stage.

Resources

- Adequate classroom or theatre space
- Large table for the jury and a chair for each actor
- Small table (for refreshments)
- Props (such as coffee pot and cups)
- BLMs 139, 140 Student Self-Assessment

There are many additional resources included in the *Teacher's Resource Book*. For those that relate to this project, see the chart at the front of this *Teacher's Manual* (pp. xviii–xxi).

Creating

As students rehearse their entrances and exits, ensure that each juror has sufficient opportunity to exhibit his or her individual attributes. If not, have them adjust the blocking.

Performing

Remind students that they are one member of a large ensemble. Up-staging other actors or breaking out of character is inappropriate.

Responding

You and the students may assess the projects using a rubric you have created. (See pages xxii–xxvi for guidance in creating rubrics.) Remind students to give each other positive, constructive feedback. Students may also use the prompts on BLMs 139, 140 to do self-assessment. Students may record their reactions to their own and to others' projects in their Theatre Notebooks. This project may also be evaluated by using the sample rubric provided on page xxv.

Project 15

Creating Stage Pictures

PREPARATION

Assignment

With a group, create a series of stage pictures that tell a story.

Objectives

- The student will be able to demonstrate an understanding of directing techniques of composition by creating stage pictures and focus through the use of tableaux.
- The student will be able to demonstrate ensemble skills.

Resources

- Classroom or theatre performance space
- Anthologies of narrative poems or short stories
- BLM 131 Alternative Assessment Rubric: Project 15
- BLMs 139, 140 Student Self-Assessment

There are many additional resources included in the *Teacher's Resource Book*. For those that relate to this project, see the chart at the front of this *Teacher's Manual* (pp. xviii–xxi).

Creating

As students begin creating stage pictures, remind them to achieve focus for each picture through body position and stage area. Encourage students to explore various ways of achieving smooth transitions from one stage picture to another.

Performing

Suggest to students that in order to maintain a body and facial freeze, they not look directly at anyone in the audience.

Responding

You and the students may assess the projects using a rubric you have created. (See pages xxii–xxvi for guidance in creating rubrics.) Remind students to give each other positive, constructive feedback. Students may also use the prompts on BLMs 139, 140 to do self-assessment. Students may record their reactions to their own and to others' projects in their Theatre Notebooks. This project, which is an alternative assessment for Chapter 5, may also be evaluated by using BLM 131.

Project 16

Developing a Director's Promptbook

P R E P A R A T I O N

Assignment

Prepare a director's promptbook.

Objectives

- The student will be able to demonstrate an understanding of the organizational structure and the components of a director's promptbook.
- The student will be able to apply and develop techniques and components for script analysis using the director's point of view.

Resources

- Anthologies of one-act plays
- Three-ring binder and six dividers
- BLMs 139, 140 Student Self-Assessment

There are many additional resources included in the *Teacher's Resource Book*. For those that relate to this project, see the chart at the front of this *Teacher's Manual* (pp. xviii–xxi).

Creating

This is an in-depth project that could be carried out over the course of several weeks. Encourage students to follow the procedure for script analysis outlined in Chapter 5, which will require reading the script several times and taking extensive notes.

Presenting

Instead of waiting until their promptbooks are completed, students could present their work at three different stages: the first, when they have completed the script analysis, character analysis, and genre/style study; the second, upon completing the ground plan and technical requirements; and the third, upon completing the blocking of two or more pages of the script.

Responding

You and the students may assess the projects using a rubric you have created. (See pages xxii–xxvi for guidance in creating rubrics.) Remind students to give each other positive, constructive feedback. Students may also use the prompts on BLMs 139, 140 to do self-assessment. Students may record their reactions to their own and to others' projects in their Theatre Notebooks.

Project 17

Producing a Play

PREPARATION

Assignment

Prepare a financial proposal for a production of a play on a given budget.

Objectives

- The student will be able to demonstrate an understanding of the process of producing a play.
- The student will be able to develop a comprehensive budget for a play and give a rationale for all funding decisions.

Resources

- Addresses and phone numbers of local theatre managers
- Catalogs of play publishers
- BLM 49 Production Budget Worksheet
- BLMs 139, 140 Student Self-Assessment

> There are many additional resources included in the *Teacher's Resource Book*. For those that relate to this project, see the chart at the front of this *Teacher's Manual* (pp. xviii–xxi).

Creating

Emphasize that budget planning is a complex and time-consuming process, one that demands precise information and accurate estimates. If students are having difficulty finding certain information, help them make educated guesses about those costs. To organize this information, students may use BLM 49.

Presenting

Suggest to students that the written proposal differ from the oral presentation. Since the proposal contains hard facts, it would typically be sent to board members before the presentation. Presentations should grab the audience's attention and appeal to their emotions.

Responding

You and the students may assess the projects using a rubric you have created. (See pages xxii–xxvi for guidance in creating rubrics.) Remind students to give each other positive, constructive feedback. Students may also use the prompts on BLMs 139, 140 to do self-assessment. Students may record their reactions to their own and to others' projects in their Theatre Notebooks.

Project 18

Designing a Set

Assignment

Design a set for a specific play.

Objectives

- The student will be able to demonstrate an understanding of the elements of scenic design by reading, analyzing, and designing a play for a specific performance space.
- The student will be able to draw a ground plan and an elevation using a scale drawing.

Resources

- Anthologies of one-act or full-length plays
- Scale drawing of local theatre performance space
- Paint, wallpaper, and/or fabric samples
- Pictures of architectural details
- Water colors or marking pens
- BLM 132 Alternative Assessment Rubric: Project 18
- BLMs 139, 140 Student Self-Assessment

> There are many additional resources included in the *Teacher's Resource Book*. For those that relate to this project, see the chart at the front of this *Teacher's Manual* (pp. xviii–xxi).

Creating

Set designers usually take their cue from the director's production concept. For this project, the student should assume the roles of both director and designer.

Presenting

In their presentations, students should first familiarize the class with the play. They should then establish the production concept underlying their design, and point out the design elements that reinforce that production concept.

Responding

You and the students may assess the projects using a rubric you have created. (See pages xxii–xxvi for guidance in creating rubrics.) Remind students to give each other positive, constructive feedback. They may also use the prompts on BLMs 139, 140 to do self-assessment. Students may record their reactions to their own and to others' projects in their Theatre Notebooks. This project, which is an alternative assessment for Chapter 6, may also be evaluated by using BLM 132.

Project 19

Reupholstering a Set Prop

PREPARATION

Assignment

Reupholster a piece of stage furniture.

Objectives

- The student will be able to demonstrate an understanding of the process of adapting furniture for use in a play.
- The student will be able to demonstrate research skills in determining the appropriate historical and cultural styles, colors, and materials in selecting and refurbishing set properties for a play.

Resources

- Chair or sofa to be reupholstered
- Upholstery fabric; decorative border (if needed)
- Padding, springs, webbing (as needed)
- Sandpaper, paint, or refinishing liquid
- Seam ripper, staple gun and staples or tack hammer and tacks
- BLMs 139, 140 Student Self-Assessment

> There are many additional resources included in the *Teacher's Resource Book*. For those that relate to this project, see the chart at the front of this *Teacher's Manual* (pp. xviii–xxi).

Creating

Remind students to ask questions about any directions they do not understand, to follow directions precisely, and to check their results by placing the completed set piece onstage and under stage lights.

Presenting

Suggest that in their presentations students discuss the decisions they had to make, the effect they wanted to achieve, and their own assessment of their success.

Responding

You and the students may assess the projects using a rubric you have created. (See pages xxii–xxvi for guidance in creating rubrics.) Remind students to give each other positive, constructive feedback. Students may also use the prompts on BLMs 139, 140 to do self-assessment. Students may record their reactions to their own and to others' projects in their Theatre Notebooks.

Project 20

Grid Transfer

PREPARATION

Assignment

Use a grid to enlarge a design.

Objectives

- The student will be able to demonstrate an understanding of the design, development, and painting of a scenery drop for a play.
- The student will be able to demonstrate the process of grid transfer as a technique for creating a scenery drop.

Resources

- Copy of image to be transferred
- Canvas, poster board, butcher paper, or a white sheet
- Sizing, light-toned paint, finish paint
- Soft pencil, ruler, charcoal, or chalk
- BLMs 139, 140 Student Self-Assessment

There are many additional resources included in the *Teacher's Resource Book*. For those that relate to this project, see the chart at the front of this *Teacher's Manual* (pp. xviii–xxi).

Creating

Indicate to students that before they can make a grid onto their material, they should square the material and mark the edges at every horizontal and vertical foot.

Presenting

After the class has viewed the finished drop, presenters might focus their comments on particular difficulties or on tips for transferring images.

Responding

You and the students may assess the projects using a rubric you have created. (See pages xxii–xxvi for guidance in creating rubrics.) Remind students to give each other positive, constructive feedback. Students may also use the prompts on BLMs 139, 140 to do self-assessment. Students may record their reactions to their own and to others' projects in their Theatre Notebooks.

Performance
Lessons

Chapter 7

Acting

PERFORMANCE

Overview

From creating to final polishing, this chapter describes a method for students to bring a specific, believable character alive onstage. The method is explained sequentially, progressing from initial script analysis to final curtain. Topics include acting style choices, rehearsal etiquette, specific kinds of rehearsals that take place throughout the process and their purpose, suggestions for character building, how to interact with technical crew members, and preparation for the performance itself. The activities and exercises provide opportunities to apply and expand upon the skills and techniques that are part of the performance process.

THE LANGUAGE OF THEATRE

cue line

fourth wall

off book

on book

presentational style

read-through

representational style

scenario

spike

stage business

Objectives

- The student will be able to demonstrate an understanding of script and character analysis and the ability to implement these skills when developing a role.

- The student will be able to demonstrate an understanding of the rehearsal process.

- The student will develop character analysis skills by building a character using internal (objectives, subtext, character biography) and external (props, costumes, makeup) techniques.

- The student will be able to understand and implement rehearsal and backstage etiquette during the production of a play.

- The student will be able to demonstrate an understanding of the various styles of acting, including farce, commedia dell'arte, social satire, comedy, tragedy, and so on.

- The student will be able to use and define appropriate theatre terminology including *pick up your cues, topping a line, open up,* and *dropping your lines.*

- The student will demonstrate an understanding of journaling with regard to character development.

Resources

- *The Book of Scenes for Aspiring Actors* (or other books of scenes)
- *The Book of Monologues for Aspiring Actors* (or other books of monologues)
- Access to rehearsal/performance space with chairs and tables
- BLMs 27, 28 Actor's Preliminary Script Analysis
- BLM 29 Actor's Script Analysis (Character)
- BLM 30 Actor's Script Analysis (Scene-by-Scene)
- BLM 31 Acting Styles
- BLM 109 Chapter 7 Test: Acting
- BLM 125 Section 3 Answer Key
- BLM 133 Alternative Assessment Rubric: Project 21
- BLMs 139, 140 Student Self-Assessment
- OVH 21 Visual Arts Link: Chapter 7 Acting

> There are many additional resources included in the *Teacher's Resource Book*. For those that relate to this chapter, see the chart at the front of this *Teacher's Manual* (pp. xviii–xxi).

Customizing

Creative Challenge

Encourage students to be as creative and as detailed as possible in both their analyses and in their performances. This may require giving students more time, greater access to technical, makeup and costuming resources, and an opportunity for a final public performance.

Links to Literature/Language Arts

Focus on the first part of the chapter, which emphasizes the literary analysis aspect of developing a character. Students could be assigned to analyze and compare a character who appears in more than one play, such as Electra, or who appears in both a play and in other literature, such as Ebenezer Scrooge.

At-Risk Students

Assign a mentor for each student to meet with throughout the rehearsal process. Mentors should be students who have had a good deal of onstage and/or backstage experience. Encourage journal entries in the Theatre Notebook detailing personal reactions and growth throughout the process.

Visual Arts Link

Using OVH 21, with *The Cheat* by Georges de la Tour, have students assume that they are one of the characters around the table and create a background for themselves. They should make up a name for the character, determine why they are there, what they want (if anything), and how they feel about other characters in the scene. Once they've built their characters, they can describe the actions they might use to make the scene believable onstage. Groups of students can then present improvisations of the scene as their characters.

Side-Coaching Tips

The following are ideas to help provide ongoing support as students do exercises and activities:

Documentation

It's important that students develop a repeatable personal process for creating a character; therefore, documentation throughout the rehearsal process is very helpful. The script analysis process outlined in BLMs 27, 28, 29, and 30 could help students document the process of creating a character. Visual documentation using photography or videotaping provides both immediate and long-term feedback. The Theatre Notebook is a natural repository for personal documentation; encourage students to use it regularly.

Observation and Imitation

Acting style is a very visual and external element of performance. Prompt students to pay particular attention to the photos and illustrations that accompany the historical profiles and the theatre outline, which may prove helpful in understanding styles. The best way to observe acting styles is to see live performances of plays in various styles. Students should be encouraged to watch a variety of performances (professional, community, filmed) and to take notes about acting styles. You might have students use BLM 31 to review acting styles.

Etiquette

Understanding the chain of command and practicing good etiquette are critical to the safety of the cast and crew and success of a performance. During the Rehearsal Etiquette exercise, students may wish to share rehearsal, backstage, or performance problem situations they have observed or experienced.

Support for Activities

The activities may be used as in-class activities, homework assignments, field trip options, or as opportunities for extra-credit work. Most of them may be accomplished in two days to a week. The Tragic Hero/Heroine activity provides an opportunity to learn one specific acting style and may require additional time.

Student Assessment

Assessment may be accomplished by measuring achievement of the objectives outlined at the beginning of this lesson plan. Students may demonstrate their success at meeting those objectives through participation in the exercises and class discussion and fulfillment of assigned activities. You may wish to create your own rubric for assessment. See pages xxii–xxvi for guidance on creating rubrics. A chapter test (BLM 109) may also be used. Project 21: Duet Performance may be used as an alternative, performance-based assessment. (BLM 133 provides a rubric for assessing student performance on this project.)

Self- and group-assessment may take the form of journaling entries in the students' Theatre Notebooks, some of which are part of the chapter exercises and activities. Other entries could address self-assessment questions (BLMs 139, 140). Finally, students might also reflect upon any constructive feedback they have received from their peers.

Kabuki

P E R F O R M A N C E

Overview

This historical profile introduces students to the powerful theatre traditions of Asia. The profile begins with a brief introduction to the three types of theatre traditional to Japan: Noh, Bunraku, and Kabuki. An in-depth description of Kabuki theatre follows, providing a detailed physical description of the Kabuki performance space, the musicians and their instruments, the chorus, costuming, and makeup. Finally, the performance style itself is explained. The profile concludes with a scene from *The Zen Substitute*, a Kabuki comedy. The Try It Out and Extension activities encourage students to hone their acting skills by practicing elements of the Kabuki acting style.

Objectives

- The student will be able to demonstrate a basic understanding of the three main traditional types of theatre in Japan.
- The student will be able to demonstrate an understanding of the style, devices, and conventions of Kabuki theatre.
- The student will be able to identify and describe appropriate scenic elements used in Kabuki theatre.
- The student will be able to identify and describe appropriate styles of costumes, accessories, and makeup for Kabuki theatre.
- The student will be able to demonstrate an understanding of the appropriate acting styles of Kabuki theatre.

Resources

- Space sufficient to rehearse and perform the scene
- Vivid colors of makeup, including white foundation and red, blue, and black grease and creme makeup.
- 1 large robe
- Fans (even handmade ones) and a sword or swordlike object (such as a yardstick)
- An Outline of Theatre History (student text, pp. 1–15)
- BLM 119 Historical Profile Test: Kabuki
- BLM 125 Section 3 Answer Key
- BLMs 139, 140 Student Self-Assessment

- BLMs 149, 150 Research Activities: Traditional Asian Theatre
- OVH 14 Diagram: Kabuki Theatre

There are many additional resources included in the *Teacher's Resource Book*. For those that relate to this historical profile, see the chart at the front of this *Teacher's Manual* (pp. xviii–xxi).

Customizing

Creative Challenge

Have the students research Japanese films on video to study the culture, actors' movements and styles, and use of sound. If possible, they should attend a Kabuki theatre performance or view one on film. Use OVH 14 to help students visualize the Kabuki theatre. The students should then rehearse and perform the scene as authentically as possible with staging, musicians, chorus, costumes, props, and stage assistants.

At-Risk Students

Focus on the familiar comedic situation and relationships found in *The Zen Substitute*. The characters of Lord Ukyo and Tarokaja can be played by male pairs, female pairs, or mixed pairs to examine how male and female roles affect the relationship. Students may also imagine and improvise the rest of the story, based on the events and characterizations introduced in this scene.

Research

Have students who would like to know more about traditional Asian theatre do one of the research activities on BLMs 149 and 150.

Side-Coaching Tips

The scene from *The Zen Substitute* includes sidenotes— comments and questions—in the margins. The following suggestions also provide ongoing support as students prepare for and perform the scene:

Makeup and Props

Students should experiment with the various ways that the makeup and props may affect facial expression, gestures, and movement. Actors may need to practice with makeup and use a mirror to understand the effect.

Stylistic Vocal Interpretation

Encourage students to experiment with the rhythm and inflection of the language—especially the chorus sections and the repeated words. The interpretation should sound different from a realistic one. The chorus should mark in their scripts and then practice common breathing points, special words to emphasize, and changes in volume or tempo. The other actors should also experiment with different emphases and volume and tempo alterations.

Alternative Activities

The following activities may be used as in-class or homework assignments or as opportunities for extra-credit work:

Playing the Opposite Gender

In Kabuki theatre, male performers do all roles. Use same-gender casts to perform the scene. Improvise the rest of the story so that men will have a chance to play women's roles and women can play men's roles. Have students discuss afterward the changes they had to make to play a character of the opposite sex and write in their Theatre Notebooks about the experience.

Create Another Scene

Using Japanese literature or another Kabuki play, direct small groups of students to create another Kabuki theatre scene to perform for the class.

Student Assessment

Assessment may be accomplished by measuring achievement of the objectives outlined at the beginning of this lesson plan. Students may demonstrate their success at meeting those objectives through participation in class discussion and in their performance of the scene from *The Zen Substitute*. They may also complete the profile test on BLM 119. You may wish to create your own rubric for assessment. See pages xxii–xxvi for guidance on creating rubrics.

Self-assessment may take the form of journaling entries in the students' Theatre Notebooks. Other entries could address self-assessment questions (BLMs 139, 140). Finally, students might also reflect upon any constructive feedback they have received from their peers.

Chapter 8

Directing & Producing

P E R F O R M A N C E

Overview

This chapter is unique in that the directing and producing skills it teaches are conveyed through the journal of Holly Sung, an imaginary high-school student who wants to become a director. The intent of this approach is to give the students a feel for what a novice director may think and experience from beginning to end during the production process, as well as to describe and teach the process itself. The journal entries describe how Holly chooses a play, assembles a production team, prepares schedules, draws up a ground plan, auditions and casts actors, directs rehearsals, and guides the cast and crew through the performances. Possible ways of approaching the material in this chapter are described in the Side-Coaching Tips section. Activities at the end of the chapter encourage students to explore the duties and skills of the director, producer, and their staffs.

THE LANGUAGE OF THEATRE

cast by type
color-blind casting
dinner theatre
director's notes
nontraditional casting
pacing
preblocking
strike
understudy

Objectives

- The student will be able to demonstrate an understanding of the specific responsibilities of the stage manager, including those involved in many aspects of production, as well as pre- and postproduction.

- The student will be able to demonstrate an understanding of the specific responsibilities of the producer, including overseeing the budget, promotion, and programs, and acquiring the rights for production.

- The student will be able to demonstrate an understanding of the specific responsibilities of the director, including play selection, preproduction, organization, scheduling, auditioning, and casting.

- The student will be able to use and define appropriate theatre vocabulary.

- The student will be able to demonstrate an understanding of directing strategies and coaching techniques, including giving notes, pacing, journaling, and communicating with technical staff and actors.

- The student will be able to understand the difference between the various types of rehearsals.
- The student will be able to understand the need for the actor's contract and for taking responsibility as part of the production process.

Resources

- BLM 49 Production Budget Worksheet
- BLM 51 Master Production Schedule Worksheet
- BLM 110 Chapter 8 Test: Directing & Producing
- BLM 125 Section 3 Answer Key
- BLM 134 Alternative Assessment Rubric: Project 24
- BLMs 139, 140 Student Self-Assessment
- OVH 22 Visual Arts Link: Chapter 8 Directing & Producing

There are many additional resources included in the *Teacher's Resource Book*. For those that relate to this chapter, see the chart at the front of this *Teacher's Manual* (pp. xviii–xxi).

Customizing

Creative Challenge

Assign students to read Neil Simon's *Star-Spangled Girl*. Based on the experiences and problems of Holly Sung, the students could create their own journal entries imagining the different types of problems they might face as directors, pertinent to this play, and how they would deal with those problems.

English-Language Learners

Pair fluent and nonfluent English speakers and have them take turns reading the journal entries to each other. Students could also be assigned to summarize and explain portions of the text to the class.

At-Risk Students

Assign students to make daily entries in their Theatre Notebooks for two weeks, using Holly Sung's journal entries as models. The entries should describe a project they are working on for class, the problems they face, how they need to interact with others to accomplish the project, and how they feel about working on the project.

Visual Arts Link

Using OVH 22, with *Akhenaton and Nefertiti* (artist unknown), have students imagine that they are directing actors who are playing these characters in a play. In small groups have them discuss such things as how they would suggest that the actors prepare for their roles. What kind of background research should the actors do? As directors, what will they do to help? What kinds of coaching tips would they give the actors in terms of movement and carriage of body to make these characters real for the audience? Have each group present its ideas to the class.

Side-Coaching Tips

The following are ideas to help provide ongoing support as students work their way through the material in this chapter:

Production Process

You might review BLMs 49 and 51 to make sure students understand these essential aspects of the production process.

Reading Strategies

Vocabulary: Since the vocabulary is imbedded in the text (not bold-faced as in other chapters), you may need to model for students the thought process used to determine meaning by context. For example, on page 316, three vocabulary words or phrases are used in the second paragraph: "A director should beware of *casting by type*. . . . But we plan to *do color-blind casting*. . . . We'll also need to cast some *understudies*. . . ." To determine the meaning, students should first read the entire paragraph. Then they might go back to each sentence. They might choose to look up the word *casting* in the glossary or a dictionary. The rest of the sentence may provide clues as to the meaning of *color-blind*. Since race and ethnicity don't matter to Holly, that must be what *color-blind* means; therefore *color-blind casting* means assigning parts in a play according to perceived talent and without regard to the playwright's instructions or traditional perceptions of race and ethnicity.

Students should also be reminded that the glossary at the back of their text explains many terms that may be unfamiliar.

Paraphrasing or Summarizing: Some of Holly's key journal entries are long and detailed. The June 6 entry about the first production meeting, the June 8 entry about preparing for auditions, and the June 20 entry about blocking a kissing scene may be particularly difficult. To be sure that students understand the content, it may be helpful to have them paraphrase or summarize the entry. Point out that paraphrasing entails restating all the author's words into one's own words, whereas summarizing is simply stating the passage's central ideas. In the case of the blocking entry, it may be helpful for a directing student to try out and then demonstrate the blocking with two student actors.

Critical Thinking Skills

Problem-Solution Chart: In order to analyze the problems that Holly faces and deals with as a novice director, it may be helpful for students to fill in a problem-solution chart. The journal entries from July 10 through July 20 present a number of problems that Holly encounters and her solutions for them. Have students identify and write down those problems and the solutions that Holly works out. Students may also discover other problems not specifically described but implied, such as how Holly and Nate persuaded Joy Chen to provide the rehearsal and performance space.

Outline/Flowchart: Holly goes through an extensive and detailed process to direct her show. Have students reread the journal and create an outline or flowchart of what Holly does: her individual homework, the staff she needs, the meetings she sets up and attends, and the different kinds of rehearsals that she conducts. The responsibilities of the producer and stage manager could also be identified from the text and made into an outline or flowchart.

Situation Improv: Using a problem that Holly faces, have students create an improv that demonstrates how Holly and her cast or crew behave with each other, how they feel in the situation, and how Holly solves the problem. For instance, have two actors re-create the phone conversation Holly has with Marcos the day after he didn't show up for rehearsal (journal entry July 11). Or, assign three actors to act out the confrontation between Lin and Darth and what Holly says and does to defuse the situation (journal entry July 19).

Support for Activities

The activities may be used as in-class activities, homework assignments, or as opportunities for extra-credit work. Most of the activities will take from two days to a week to complete. For the Community Resources activity, you might invite a staff member from a local theatre group to visit your class as a guest speaker.

Student Assessment

Assessment may be accomplished by measuring achievement of the objectives outlined at the beginning of this lesson plan. Students may demonstrate their success at meeting those objectives through participation in class discussion and fulfillment of assigned activities. You may wish to create your own rubric for assessment. See pages xxii–xxvi for guidance on creating rubrics. A chapter test (BLM 110) may also be used. Project 24: Stage Composition and Emphasis may be used as an alternative, performance-based assessment. (BLM 134 provides a rubric for assessing student performance on this project.)

Self- and group-assessment may take the form of journaling entries in the students' Theatre Notebooks, some of which are part of the chapter activities. Other entries could address self-assessment questions (BLMs 139, 140). Finally, students might also reflect upon any constructive feedback they have received from their peers.

Chekhov

PERFORMANCE

Overview

The historical profile on Anton Chekhov describes the life and work of the Russian playwright, whose work helped usher in modern acting and directing techniques. Included in the profile are a brief biography of Chekhov, a summary of his writings, a discussion on the movement from Romanticism to realism in theatre, a description of costuming and stage movement at the time, and an overview of Stanislavski's work and the Moscow Art Theatre. The profile concludes with a scene from *Uncle Vanya,* and the Try It Out and Extension activities encourage students to apply their directing skills to this scene.

Objectives

- The student will be able to demonstrate a basic knowledge of the life and works of Anton Chekhov.
- The student will be able to demonstrate an understanding of the basic differences between Romanticism and realism as the two dominant cultural movements in the 1800s and early 1900s.
- The student will be able to identify and describe basic styles of costumes and movement in the theatre during Chekhov's professional life.
- The student will be able to demonstrate a basic knowledge of the Moscow Art Theatre and its relationship to Chekhov.
- The student will be able to demonstrate an understanding of both the acting styles envisioned by Chekhov and those used by the Moscow Art Theatre.

Resources

- Space sufficient to rehearse and perform the scene
- An Outline of Theatre History (student text, pp. 1–15)
- BLM 120 Historical Profile Test: Chekhov
- BLM 125 Section 3 Answer Key
- BLMs 139, 140 Student Self-Assessment
- BLMs 151, 152 Research Activities: Theatre in the 1800s

There are many additional resources included in the *Teacher's Resource Book.* For those that relate to this historical profile, see the chart at the front of this *Teacher's Manual* (pp. xviii–xxi).

Customizing

Creative Challenge

Assign students to read *An Actor Prepares* by Konstantin Stanislavski. The student director and actors should discuss Stanislavski's approach and use it to prepare and present the scene from *Uncle Vanya* or a scene from another of Chekhov's plays.

At-Risk Students

After a discussion of the differences between Stanislavski's approach and Chekhov's intention, have students relate this difference of opinion to their own lives. When have they been interpreted differently from what they had intended? Why do they think this happened?

Links to Literature/Language Arts

Have students read the entire play, *Uncle Vanya*, and other works by Chekhov to learn more about his literary style and themes. Students should record their thoughts on Chekhov and his works in their Theatre Notebooks.

Research

Have students who want to learn more about the theatre of Chekhov's time do one of the research activities on BLMs 151 and 152.

Side-Coaching Tips

The scene from *Uncle Vanya* includes sidenotes—comments and questions—in the margins. The following suggestions also provide ongoing support as directing students prepare their actors to perform the scene:

Comic Timing

Chekhov's work is neither heavy-handed farce nor comedy of manners. The humor should arise from the reality of the situation, the words not spoken, and the flaws of the characters. Because the comedy is sometimes subtle, student directors must pay particular attention to the timing of actors' lines, pauses, entrances, and pickups.

Subtext

Because Chekhov conveys so much in what characters imply, student directors and actors must pay particular attention to what is contained in the subtext. Improvisation and discussion are valuable tools for exploring character relationships and motivation.

Alternative Activities

The following activities may be used as in-class or homework assignments or as opportunities for extra-credit work:

Changing the Style

Sometimes, in order to communicate what they feel is its message, directors alter the style of a play from its original production. What would happen if Chekhov's play were set in the present time in the United States? What would happen if the characters expressed what they were really thinking as asides to the audience? What would happen if the comedy was physicalized? What would happen if a Romantic style was used? Have directing students experiment with changing an aspect of the style in the *Uncle Vanya* scene. They should have their actors perform the scene once in its original style and once with the changes that they have imposed on it. Directing students should observe the effects of the change on the audience and the actors. They should identify the theme of Chekhov's play and decide whether it is still conveyed with the change in style. Students should record their observations about this experimentation in their Theatre Notebooks.

Comparison with David Mamet

David Mamet, a well-known American playwright, has created the adaptation of Chekhov's play used in the text. Assign students to compare Mamet's writing style in the Chekhov scene with his style in a scene from one of his own original plays, such as *American Buffalo* or *Glengarry Glen Ross*. Students should consider the theme, the rhythm of the language and dialogue, the types of characters, and the situations in which they find themselves. Students could write a summary of their conclusions in their Theatre Notebooks.

Student Assessment

Assessment may be accomplished by measuring achievement of the objectives outlined at the beginning of this lesson plan. Students may demonstrate their success at meeting those objectives through participation in class discussion and in their role in the performance of the scene from *Uncle Vanya*. They may also complete the profile test on BLM 120. You may wish to create your own rubric for assessment. See pages xxii–xxvi for guidance on creating rubrics.

Self-assessment may take the form of journaling entries in the students' Theatre Notebooks. Other entries could address self-assessment questions (BLMs 139, 140). Finally, students might also reflect upon any constructive feedback they have received from their peers.

Chapter 9

Technical Theatre

P E R F O R M A N C E

Overview

In this chapter, all final technical preparations for a show are described from setups to tech and dress rehearsals to performance. The tasks to be accomplished before performance are detailed, and guidelines for tech and dress rehearsals, running the show, and postproduction tasks are provided. The stage manager's duties during this time period are also described. Skills emphasized are organizing, finishing tasks, managing details, and performing calmly under pressure. Instructions for returning the stage, storage, and work areas to normal after the production closes complete the chapter. The activities allow students to develop skills in the various tech areas, including the handling of scenery, props, lighting, sound, costumes, makeup, and front-of-house duties.

Objectives

- The student will be able to demonstrate an understanding and working knowledge of the basic scenic requirements needed during technical rehearsals, performance, and postproduction, including shifting scenery, running flats, storing flats, handling heavy scenery, and attending to safety concerns.

- The student will be able to demonstrate an understanding and working knowledge of sound production during setup, technical rehearsals, performance, and postproduction, including electronics, cue sheets, and safety concerns.

- The student will be able to demonstrate an understanding and working knowledge of makeup techniques, clean-up procedures, and safety concerns.

- The student will be able to demonstrate an understanding and working knowledge of stage lighting during technical rehearsals, dress rehearsals, performance, and postproduction, including hanging, angling, and focusing lights; installing gels; running lights; developing and using cue sheets; and safety concerns.

- The student will be able to demonstrate an understanding and working knowledge of the organization and maintenance of props during setup, technical rehearsals, dress rehearsals, performance, and postproduction.

- The student will be able to demonstrate an understanding and working knowledge of the organization and maintenance of costumes during setup, technical rehearsals, performance, and postproduction.

THE LANGUAGE OF THEATRE

boom or **boomerang**
   or **lighting tree**
call
cyclorama or **cyc**
dry tech
fly
gobo
grip
paper tech
rigging
wagon

- The student will be able to demonstrate an understanding of the basic techniques of dyeing, decorating, and texturizing costumes and adapting commercial patterns.
- The student will be able to demonstrate an understanding and working knowledge of the organization and maintenance of makeup during setup, technical rehearsals, performance, and postproduction.
- The student will be able to demonstrate an understanding and working knowledge of the role and responsibilities of the stage manager during setup, technical rehearsals, performance, and postproduction.
- The student will be able to use and define appropriate technical theatre vocabulary.

Resources

- Performance space, props, and scenery as detailed in chapter
- Lighting control system, instruments, and rigging supplies as detailed in chapter
- Sound control system and recording and playback equipment and supplies as detailed in chapter
- Costume shop, tools, and supplies as detailed in chapter
- Makeup supplies and facilities as detailed in chapter
- BLM 6 Job Shadow Agreement
- BLM 92 Makeup Plan
- BLM 111 Chapter 9 Test: Technical Theatre
- BLM 125 Section 3 Answer Key
- BLM 135 Alternative Assessment Rubric: Project 29
- BLMs 139, 140 Student Self-Assessment
- OVH 23 Visual Arts Link: Chapter 9 Technical Theatre

There are many additional resources included in the *Teacher's Resource Book*. For those that relate to this chapter, see the chart at the front of this *Teacher's Manual* (pp. xviii–xxi).

Customizing

Classrooms with Limited Resources

Focus on the overall organization skills needed to rehearse and run a show. If students have personal access to equipment, such as sound-recording equipment or sewing machines, encourage them to work independently. If your performance space will be the classroom, students may still utilize as many technical elements as the space, budget, and their ingenuity and resources will allow.

Students with Disabilities

Because there is such great variety in the technical skills and tasks needed to stage a show, everyone can contribute. Students may be encouraged to work in the area that best suits their needs and abilities. For instance, students with visual disabilities could work more extensively with sound, persons with physical disabilities could manage the prop table, and so on.

Creative Challenge

Makeup students might like to try out their skills in a "makeup contest." As a class, you and your students can decide upon the criteria for such a contest. For example, you might decide upon categories, such as "best alien face," "scariest face," "best animal face," and so on. All students could be allotted a limited time to apply the makeup, after which the rest of the class could choose the winner.

Visual Arts Link

Using OVH 23, with *Gospel Singer* by Daniel Nevins, discuss with students how they could use makeup to reshape an actor's face to resemble the woman in the painting. Ask a student from the class to volunteer as a model, and then have the other students work with partners to prepare a makeup plan (using BLM 92), which they would use to alter the shape of the model's face. Partners can present their makeup plan to the class. If time permits, have the model apply makeup according to one of the makeup plans.

Side-Coaching Tips

The following are ideas to help provide ongoing support as students do activities:

Practice

Practice reduces panic and stress because students know their jobs well and learn how to work together as a team. A practiced action, such as a well-choreographed set change, provides a familiar structure that often prevails in pressure situations or when common sense fails.

Lists

Lists are very important. They provide the most organized way to keep track of a multitude of details. Everyone should have and use a performance checklist of some type.

Keeping Focused

During the chaos of tech week or the unexpected crises that may happen onstage at any time, students can contribute to a safe and successful show by keeping on task, knowing their jobs well, and remaining relaxed and flexible. Encourage directing students to include time in their rehearsal schedules for all participants—not just the actors—to do relaxation and focusing exercises.

Finishing the Job

Explain how students may have trouble shifting gears and returning to "normal" life when a production run has ended. Encourage them to view postproduction tasks—cleaning up; returning borrowed resources; storing tools, equipment, props, and costumes; and restoring stage and work areas—as part of a "winding-down" ritual that can help them make the transition.

Support for Activities

The activities may be used as in-class activities, homework assignments, or as opportunities for extra-credit work. By this time, students have begun to identify their interests and to specialize in their skills. The activities provide more advanced tasks to further those skills. Good organization skills must be developed early on and cannot be overemphasized. The Tech Rehearsal, Dress Rehearsal, and Run of the Show activities provide advance practice for potential problem situations. The Job Shadow—Tailor activity may continue through the semester or year. Be sure to review with students the guidelines for job shadowing on BLM 6.

Student Assessment

Assessment may be accomplished by measuring achievement of the objectives outlined at the beginning of this lesson plan. Students may demonstrate their success at meeting those objectives through participation in class discussion and fulfillment of assigned activities. You may wish to create your own rubric for assessment. See pages xxii–xxvi for guidance on creating rubrics. A chapter test (BLM 111) may also be used. Project 29: Analyzing Scene Changes may be used as an alternative, performance-based assessment. (BLM 135 provides a rubric for assessing student performance on this project.)

Self- and group-assessment may take the form of journaling entries in the students' Theatre Notebooks, some of which are part of the chapter activities. Other entries could address self-assessment questions (BLMs 139, 140). Finally, students might also reflect upon any constructive feedback they have received from their peers.

Duet Performance

P E R F O R M A N C E

Assignment

With a partner, prepare and perform a brief dramatic scene.

Objectives

- The student will be able to demonstrate an understanding of the criteria for script selection and suitability.
- The student will be able to demonstrate an understanding of character analysis and development.
- The student will be able to demonstrate through cooperative learning the basics of acting and rehearsal techniques.

Resources

- *The Book of Scenes for Aspiring Actors* (or other books of scenes)
- Rehearsal and performance space
- BLM 133 Alternative Assessment Rubric: Project 21
- BLMs 139, 140 Student Self-Assessment

> There are many additional resources included in the *Teacher's Resource Book*. For those that relate to this project, see the chart at the front of this *Teacher's Manual* (pp. xviii–xxi).

Creating

You may ask students to turn in a rehearsal schedule to make sure that they are on target with their rehearsal times and preparations. You may also set a deadline for script selection and ask to be informed of the script choice when it's made.

Performing

Encourage students to warm up and focus before performing. Allow enough time for students to set up their scenes and complete their performance without feeling stressed or rushed.

Responding

You and the students may assess the projects using a rubric you have created. (See pages xxii–xxvi for guidance in creating rubrics.) Remind students to give each other positive, constructive feedback. Students may also use the prompts on BLMs 139, 140 to do self-assessment. Students may record their reactions to their own and to others' projects in their Theatre Notebooks. This project, which is an alternative assessment for Chapter 7, may also be evaluated by using BLM 133.

Project 22

Characterization Using Animal Traits

PERFORMANCE

Assignment

Perform a character incorporating traits observed in an animal.

Objectives

- The student will be able to demonstrate an understanding of the criteria for script selection and suitability.
- The student will be able to demonstrate an understanding of character analysis and utilize observation skills for character development.

Resources

- *The Book of Scenes for Aspiring Actors* (or other books of scenes)
- *The Book of Monologues for Aspiring Actors* (or other books of monologues)
- Rehearsal and performance space
- Costumes and props (as needed)
- BLMs 139, 140 Student Self-Assessment

There are many additional resources included in the *Teacher's Resource Book*. For those that relate to this project, see the chart at the front of this *Teacher's Manual* (pp. xviii–xxi).

Creating

Students should utilize a good portion of this time in careful observation and also in physically and vocally exploring many different possibilities. This is the time for students to experiment and expand their comfort zones—the range and types of movements with which students feel comfortable. Encourage students to write down their observations in their Theatre Notebooks.

Performing

After experimenting, students need to commit to their physical and vocal choices. This means rehearsing carefully and refining to the point that the externals of the characterization become second nature.

Responding

You and the students may assess the projects using a rubric you have created. (See pages xxii–xxvi for guidance in creating rubrics.) Remind students to give each other positive, constructive feedback. Students may also use the prompts on BLMs 139, 140 to do self-assessment. Students may record their reactions to their own and to others' projects in their Theatre Notebooks.

Project 23

Commedia dell'Arte Performance

P E R F O R M A N C E

Assignment

With an ensemble, improvise a commedia dell'arte performance based on a given scenario, or plot outline.

Objectives

- The student will be able to utilize improvisation to develop plot outlines, or scenarios, while demonstrating ensemble and rehearsal skills.
- The student will be able to explore and examine the commedia dell'arte style through movement, gestures, and improvisation.

Resources

- Rehearsal and performance space
- Appropriate costumes and props
- BLMs 139, 140 Student Self-Assessment

There are many additional resources included in the *Teacher's Resource Book*. For those that relate to this project, see the chart at the front of this *Teacher's Manual* (pp. xviii–xxi).

Creating

The physical nature of the commedia characters is essential to the comedy. Students should work carefully to create distinct physical characteristics. Those characteristics may serve as a springboard to develop some of the comic routines.

Performing

As an ensemble, the students need to be comfortable with each other and flexible during performance. Sometimes the funniest moments occur spontaneously. Students need to be prepared to incorporate any unplanned creative choices that may develop.

Responding

You and the students may assess the projects using a rubric you have created. (See pages xxii–xxvi for guidance in creating rubrics.) Remind students to give each other positive, constructive feedback. Students may also use the prompts on BLMs 139, 140 to do self-assessment. Students may record their reactions to their own and to others' projects in their Theatre Notebooks.

Project 24

Stage Composition and Emphasis

PERFORMANCE

Assignment

Create a series of tableaux with various composition emphases.

Objectives

- The student will be able to demonstrate an understanding of balance and focus in stage composition.
- The student will be able to demonstrate an understanding of direct emphasis, duoemphasis, secondary emphasis, and diversified emphasis.

Resources

- Rehearsal and performance space
- Props, lighting, sound, and costumes (as needed)
- BLM 134 Alternative Assessment Rubric: Project 24
- BLMs 139, 140 Student Self-Assessment

> There are many additional resources included in the *Teacher's Resource Book*. For those that relate to this project, see the chart at the front of this *Teacher's Manual* (pp. xviii–xxi).

Creating

Directing students should ask their actors to be patient when rehearsing and positioning. Although directing students may have done their homework properly, discrepancies between what works on paper and what works onstage can still occur.

Performing

Directing students need to take time and make sure that they and their actors are well prepared. The performance should not begin until the director is assured that all technical elements are in place and everyone is ready. Remind directing students that the transitions between compositions should happen smoothly, quickly, and quietly.

Responding

You and the students may assess the projects using a rubric you have created. (See pages xxii–xxvi for guidance on creating rubrics.) Remind students to give each other positive, constructive feedback. Students may also use the prompts on BLMs 139, 140 to do self-assessment. Students may record their reactions to their own and to others' projects in their Theatre Notebooks. This project, which is an alternative assessment for Chapter 8, may also be evaluated by using BLM 134.

Dealing with a Difficult Actor

P E R F O R M A N C E

Assignment

Role-play solutions or ways to handle personnel problems.

Objectives

- The student will be able to demonstrate an understanding of role-playing as a tool for teaching conflict resolution.
- The student will be able to explore, examine, and develop communication skills.

Resources

- Space to perform and discuss the role play
- BLMs 139, 140 Student Self-Assessment

> There are many additional resources included in the *Teacher's Resource Book*. For those that relate to this project, see the chart at the front of this *Teacher's Manual* (pp. xviii–xxi).

Creating

Students need to take the role play seriously and fill in as much detail as they can to re-create the situation. The director and actors involved need to respond and react as honestly as possible.

Performing

While performing the role play, students shouldn't take any easy ways out but follow the role play through to its conclusion and remain in character. Just as most situations in real life don't have quick, convenient answers, neither should a role play.

Responding

You and the students may assess the projects using a rubric you have created. (See pages xxii–xxvi for guidance in creating rubrics.) Remind students to give each other positive, constructive feedback. Students may also use the prompts on BLMs 139, 140 to do self-assessment. Students may record their reactions to their own and to others' projects in their Theatre Notebooks. If one or more of the role plays raise further issues that merit discussion, you may wish to set aside some time for additional conversation about what happened.

Project 26

Directing a One-Act Play

PERFORMANCE

Assignment

Direct a one-act play.

Objectives

- The student will be able to demonstrate an understanding of the criteria for script selection, suitability, and analysis.
- The student will be able to demonstrate the basics of directing, blocking, and rehearsing techniques, as well as an understanding of developing and keeping a director's promptbook.
- The student will be able to demonstrate an understanding of the audition and casting process.

Resources

- Anthologies of one-act plays
- Rehearsal and performance space
- Minimal set, props, and costumes
- BLMs 139, 140 Student Self-Assessment

There are many additional resources included in the *Teacher's Resource Book*. For those that relate to this project, see the chart at the front of this *Teacher's Manual* (pp. xviii–xxi).

Creating

Directing students need to maintain good communication with you throughout the production process. Scheduling progress meetings at specific points in the production process or attending specific rehearsals and production meetings may help facilitate communication.

Performing

The performance itself is an opportunity for the director to step back and take a fresh look at the production. Directing students should be encouraged to observe how the audience responds to the performance and how that response affects the actors. Student directors should also record in their Theatre Notebooks what it felt like to watch the result of their efforts and to see their shows being performed.

Responding

You and the students may assess the projects using a rubric you have created. (See pages xxii–xxvi for guidance in creating rubrics.) Remind students to give each other positive, constructive feedback. Students may also use the prompts on BLMs 139, 140 to do self-assessment. Students may record their reactions to their own and to others' projects in their Theatre Notebooks. This project may also be evaluated by using the sample rubric provided on page xxvi.

Project 27

Creating a Gobo

PERFORMANCE

Assignment

Create a design and construct a gobo for a specific lighting instrument.

Objectives

- The student will be able to demonstrate an understanding of designing and creating a gobo.
- The student will be able to demonstrate an understanding of lighting design utilizing basic special effects.

Resources

- Lighting equipment, such as an ellipsoidal reflector spotlight
- Sheet of aluminum or stainless steel or a heavyweight disposable roasting pan or pie plate
- Tools, such as a pair of scissors, file, chisel, utility knife, Dremel tool, and coping saw
- BLMs 139, 140 Student Self-Assessment

> There are many additional resources included in the *Teacher's Resource Book*. For those that relate to this project, see the chart at the front of this *Teacher's Manual* (pp. xviii–xxi).

Creating

Encourage students to watch for very striking or unusual lighting effects in nature and to be observant of light and shadow in artificial lighting situations. Ask them to think about what kinds of objects create what kinds of shadows and how the position of the light source affects the shadow. Encourage them to record their observations in their Theatre Notebooks using sketches and written descriptions.

Presenting

The student should make sure that the gobo creates the intended effect. If not, discuss as a class what effect is created and if the gobo can be altered to achieve its original intent.

Responding

You and the students may assess the projects using a rubric you have created. (See pages xxii–xxvi for guidance in creating rubrics.) Remind students to give each other positive, constructive feedback. Students may also use the prompts on BLMs 139, 140 to do self-assessment. Students may record their reactions to their own and to others' projects in their Theatre Notebooks.

Making a Show Tape

P E R F O R M A N C E

Assignment

Make a show tape for a one-act play or a scene from a play.

Objectives

- The student will be able to demonstrate an understanding of script analysis for sound design.
- The student will be able to design, develop, and create a sound tape for a specific play, as well as rehearse and perform the play utilizing a sound cue sheet.

Resources

- Anthologies of one-act plays
- *The Book of Scenes for Aspiring Actors* (or other books of scenes)
- Performance space with playback capabilities
- Reel-to-reel tape recorder and audiotape
- Splicing tools
- BLM 63 Sound Basics
- BLM 64 Collecting Sounds
- BLMs 139, 140 Student Self-Assessment

There are many additional resources included in the *Teacher's Resource Book*. For those that relate to this project, see the chart at the front of this *Teacher's Manual* (pp. xviii–xxi).

Creating

Once students have determined the sounds that are needed, they should experiment with different ways of making and recording the sounds. Sometimes a sound effects tape is the best answer, while in other cases, actually going out into the environment to record the sound works best. At times, sounds must be physically created and recorded by the student. Suggest that students organize the sounds they need on a chart listing recorded, created, and found sounds. You might give students BLMs 63 and 64 to help them do this project.

Presenting

Practicing beforehand with the actors is very important. The actors' input may lead to altering the way a sound is cued or timed or its overall volume.

Responding

You and the students may assess the projects using a rubric you have created. (See pages xxii–xxvi for guidance in creating rubrics.) Remind students to give each other positive, constructive feedback. Students may also use the prompts on BLMs 139, 140 to do self-assessment. Students may record their reactions to their own and to others' projects in their Theatre Notebooks.

Project 29

Analyzing Scene Changes

PERFORMANCE

Assignment

Analyze the scene changes needed for a full-length, multiset play.

Objectives

- The student will be able to analyze the technical capabilities of a given theatre for a multiple-set production.
- The student will be able to demonstrate an understanding of running-crew responsibilities and developing assignments for a multiple-set production.

Resources

- Anthologies of plays
- Performance space
- BLM 135 Alternative Assessment Rubric: Project 29
- BLMs 139, 140 Student Self-Assessment

There are many additional resources included in the *Teacher's Resource Book*. For those that relate to this project, see the chart at the front of this *Teacher's Manual* (pp. xviii–xxi).

Creating

The student should do a reality check periodically to make sure that what they plan on paper will actually work onstage. Physically walking through and seeing the space may change some assumptions. Space required for crew members to move items will take more space than for storing the items. There must also be sufficient space for actors to get onstage efficiently.

Presenting

Students should remember that crew members may not all have the same strength, agility, or stamina. It may helpful for students to try out some of their plans beforehand to make sure their expectations are realistic.

Responding

You and the students may assess the projects using a rubric you have created. (See pages xxii–xxvi for guidance in creating rubrics.) Remind students to give each other positive, constructive feedback. Students may also use the prompts on BLMs 139, 140 to do self-assessment. Students may record their reactions to their own and to others' projects in their Theatre Notebooks. This project, which is an alternative assessment for Chapter 9, may also be evaluated by using BLM 135.

Project 30

Old-Age Makeup

PERFORMANCE

Assignment

Create old-age makeup for a specific actor playing a specific part.

Objectives

- The student will be able to demonstrate preparation, application, and removal techniques for old-age theatrical makeup.
- The student will be able to demonstrate an understanding of character analysis and theatrical makeup by designing old-age makeup for a specific character and actor.

Resources

- Anthologies of plays
- *The Book of Scenes for Aspiring Actors* (or other books of scenes)
- *The Book of Monologues for Aspiring Actors* (or other books of monologues)
- Work area that is properly lit
- Makeup kit
- BLMs 139, 140 Student Self-Assessment

> There are many additional resources included in the *Teacher's Resource Book*. For those that relate to this project, see the chart at the front of this *Teacher's Manual* (pp. xviii–xxi).

Creating

The student makeup artist and actor should choose a character and a type of face that is very interesting to them. The choice should have enough complexity to be challenging but still be manageable enough so that students can create and re-create the look.

Presenting

Stress the importance of documenting the work with photos or sketches and building a portfolio. In this way, students can begin to build upon what they have already learned and accomplished.

Responding

You and the students may assess the projects using a rubric you have created. (See pages xxii–xxvi for guidance in creating rubrics.) Remind students to give each other positive, constructive feedback. Students may also use the prompts on BLMs 139, 140 to do self-assessment. Students may record their reactions to their own and to others' projects in their Theatre Notebooks.

Specialization
Lessons

Acting

SPECIALIZATION

Overview

Chapter 10 takes a detailed look at several acting specialties. It covers the acting techniques appropriate to a Reader's Theatre performance; realistic and stylized movement; kinds of movement, such as mime and stage combat; the vocal specialties of dialect and accent; the use of masks to convey character and emotion; and acting techniques for musical theatre, film and TV, and multimedia and performance art.

Exercises and activities enable students to practice these specialized acting techniques.

THE LANGUAGE OF THEATRE

choreographer
mime
multimedia
musical theatre
principal
production number
Reader's Theatre
screenplay
stage combat

Objectives

- The student will be able to demonstrate an understanding of the differences and similarities between a dramatic play and other media or venues, such as Reader's Theatre, film, TV, and musical theatre.

- The student will be able to demonstrate an understanding of the various styles of movement for characterizations and the differences between literal realistic movement, enlarged realistic movement, stylized movement, and symbolic movement.

- The student will be able to demonstrate through performance an understanding of basic mime principles.

- The student will be able to demonstrate through performance an understanding of basic stage combat principles and safety rules.

- The student will be able to demonstrate and develop vocal variety and flexibility for characterization through the use of accents and dialects.

- The student will be able to demonstrate an understanding of the process of auditioning and performing for the camera.

- The student will be able to use and define appropriate theatre/multimedia terminology including vocabulary used in film and TV.

Resources

- Well-lit performance space
- Practice mats
- Chairs or stools
- Lecterns or stands

- Dialect audio- or videotapes
- Materials to make simple masks
- Mirrors
- Video recording/playback equipment
- BLM 6 Job Shadow Agreement
- BLMs 33, 34 Choreography
- BLM 112 Chapter 10 Test: Acting
- BLM 126 Section 4 Answer Key
- BLM 136 Alternative Assessment Rubric: Project 31
- BLMs 139, 140 Student Self-Assessment
- OVH 24 Visual Arts Link: Chapter 10 Acting

> There are many additional resources included in the *Teacher's Resource Book*. For those that relate to this chapter, see the chart at the front of this *Teacher's Manual* (pp. xviii–xxi).

Customizing

Links to Literature/Language Arts
Allow interested students to select material for a Reader's Theatre production from literature they are studying in their language arts classes. After adapting and rehearsing this material, students could perform for a number of language arts classes and lead discussions with them about the adaptations. Afterward, they can reflect upon this process in their Theatre Notebooks.

English-Language Learners
Using masks they have made and speaking in their own language, students may develop and present a one- or two-minute character monologue. Have the class discuss what kind of character is being conveyed. Then ask students to repeat or summarize the presentation in English.

Creative Challenge
Encourage students to practice using a videotape recorder in their free time. They might tape their family members or friends, using a variety of shots and angles. After viewing the tape, students should reflect in their Theatre Notebooks on the overall effect created by the different shots.

Visual Arts Link
Using OVH 24, with *Bridge Across the Moon* by Yashima Gakutei, have students imagine that this painting is a scene from a musical and that they are one of the characters in the scene—the oarsman, the man or the woman on the boat, or the person standing on the bridge. Explain that in this scene their character is about to break into song. Have them write a brief paragraph that explains what their song is about. Point out that they will first have to create some general background information—what is going on in the scene and what their character is doing—to give their song a context. Suggest that they look closely at details in the painting that might suggest this information as well as a subject for a song.

Side-Coaching Tips

Rehearsing Reader's Theatre

Scripts in Reader's Theatre are usually inserted into folders or three-ring notebooks. To avoid distracting noise during performances, have readers practice the silent turning of script pages. Suggest that if the script permits, readers stagger the timing of page turnings.

Presenting Reader's Theatre

Remind students participating in Reader's Theatre not to specifically look at the audience unless directed to do so. The director may identify focal points in the performance space for specific events or places in the script to unify the cast for moments when group focus is needed.

Improving Movement

Movement should enhance a characterization, not call attention to itself. Stress to students that movement must be motivated by the text, the subtext, and the situation.

Mime Makeup

Mimes use makeup as a mask. Have students study the pictures in the text, noting where professional mimes apply the traditional whiteface makeup and what additions they make to it in order to create a character. If time and resources permit, have students design and apply a personal mime mask.

Timing a Fight

Remind students that a stage fight is a matter of timing and total concentration. Suggest that students practice counting together during fight scenes to establish specific times for each movement in a fight sequence.

Using Vocal Variety

Using audio and videotape tapes, plus a written text of what students are hearing, introduce students to various dialects and accents. Have students repeat the sound of individual vowels and consonants, as well as vocal pitch and rhythm patterns until they can replicate them exactly.

Breaking into Song

The transition from dialogue to song will seem awkward if the action comes to an abrupt halt. The performer should continue the subtext and the life of the character from the dialogue through the musical introduction and during all musical moments, including those when the performer is not singing.

Brainstorming Multimedia Themes

For students putting together an individual or group multimedia presentation, suggest that they begin with an idea or theme, and then build a word web. Once they have those related words, they should brainstorm objects, techniques, and specific multimedia—slides, posters, sounds, artifacts—that would convey their theme.

Support for Activities

The activities may be used as in-class activities, homework assignments, or as opportunities for extra-credit work. Most can be completed in one or two days. The Job Shadow—Radio Announcer activity may continue through the semester or year. Be sure to review with students the guidelines for job shadowing on BLM 6. To help students do the activity on creating a dance number, you might suggest that they review some of the dance steps outlined in BLMs 33 and 34.

Student Assessment

Assessment may be accomplished by measuring achievement of the objectives outlined at the beginning of this lesson plan. Students may demonstrate their success at meeting those objectives through participation in the exercises and class discussion and fulfillment of assigned activities. You may wish to create your own rubric for assessment. See pages xxii–xxvi for guidance on creating rubrics. A chapter test (BLM 112) may also be used. Project 31: Using an Accent may be used as an alternative, performance-based assessment. (BLM 136 provides a rubric for assessing student performance on this project.)

Self- and group-assessment may take the form of journaling entries in the students' Theatre Notebooks, some of which are part of the chapter exercises and activities. Other entries could address self-assessment questions (BLMs 139, 140). Finally, students might also reflect upon any constructive feedback they have received from their peers.

Beckett

SPECIALIZATION

Overview

This historical profile briefly summarizes Beckett's life and chief accomplishments; discusses the philosophical and theatrical characteristics of the artistic movement known as theatre of the absurd; and describes Beckett's contribution to the movement. Students analyze and perform a scene from Beckett's *Waiting for Godot*. The Try It Out and Extension activities allow students to practice acting techniques and theatrical devices that will strengthen their skills as actors.

Objectives

- The student will be able to demonstrate a basic knowledge of the life and works of Samuel Beckett.
- The student will be able to demonstrate a basic knowledge of the themes, devices, and major playwrights associated with the theatre of the absurd.
- The student will be able to demonstrate through performance an understanding of the acting challenges that are associated with the theatre of the absurd.

Resources

- Space sufficient to rehearse and perform the scene
- Hats, overcoats, boots
- Prop "tree" (a hat stand would work)
- An Outline of Theatre History (student text, pp. 1–15)
- BLM 121 Historical Profile Test: Beckett
- BLM 126 Section 4 Answer Key
- BLMs 139, 140 Student Self-Assessment
- BLMs 153, 154 Research Activities: Theatre of the Absurd

There are many additional resources included in the *Teacher's Resource Book*. For those that relate to this historical profile, see the chart at the front of this *Teacher's Manual* (pp. xviii–xxi).

Customizing

At-Risk Students

Invite students to act out different kinds of waiting, for example, waiting for a bus, waiting for a loved one to come out of surgery, waiting for a phone call from a boyfriend or girlfriend, and so on. How do their physical movements, gestures, and expressions convey their emotions as they wait? Then have students compare and contrast these kinds of waiting with what happens in the scene from *Waiting for Godot*. How might Vladimir and Estragon physically express the act of waiting?

Research

Have students who would like to know more about the theatre of the absurd do one of the research activities on BLMs 153 and 154.

Side-Coaching Tips

The scene from *Waiting for Godot* includes sidenotes—comments and questions—in the margins. The following suggestions also provide ongoing support as students perform the scene:

Finding the Character

Before performing this scene, remind the actors to analyze the characters and create a biographical profile. Have the actors share their character research with each other and discuss if they have created enough differences to make each of these two characters unique to an audience. They should make any necessary adjustments, rehearse, and then perform the scene for the class. The actors may lead a class discussion focusing on their character choices. The actors might reflect on this characterization process in their Theatre Notebooks.

Using the Space

Beckett includes very few stage movement directions, leaving the actors and director to originate appropriate gestures and movements. To avoid a static scene, encourage the actors to use the entire performance space, including various levels and planes, while maintaining focus on the established characteristics of their characters.

Creating Visual Humor

For students puzzled by the term *vaudeville routines* (page 430 in the student text), remind them of the physical humor and word play associated with actors who use this type of humor such as the Three Stooges, Charlie Chaplin, Bud Abbott and Lou Costello, and Stan Laurel and Oliver Hardy. Then suggest that the actors devise physical stage business for Vladimir or Estragon that can be included either during a short series of speeches or during one of the many pauses. Point out that such business will not grow out of hints in the script; that it must be rehearsed carefully; and that it should be funny.

Alternative Activities

The following activities may be used as in-class or homework assignments or as opportunities for extra-credit work:

Changing the Pace

After one or two pairs of students have presented their scene, have them choose a one-minute section of the scene and enact it at a slower or faster pace; alternately, they may bring in another prop and play with it. Discuss how these changes affect the acting.

Pursuing Absurdity

After students have presented their Beckett scene, introduce students to a short excerpt from another theatre of the absurd drama, such as Edward Albee's *The American Dream* or Eugène Ionesco's *The Bald Soprano*. Working in small groups, have students compare the scene's style and acting demands to those of the scene from *Waiting for Godot*. Have them write their conclusions in their Theatre Notebooks.

Student Assessment

Assessment may be accomplished by measuring achievement of the objectives outlined at the beginning of this lesson plan. Students may demonstrate their success at meeting those objectives through participation in class discussion and in their performance of the scene from *Waiting for Godot*. They may also complete the profile test on BLM 121. You may wish to create your own rubric for assessment. See pages xxii–xxvi for guidance on creating rubrics.

Self-assessment may take the form of journaling entries in the students' Theatre Notebooks. Other entries could address self-assessment questions (BLMs 139, 140). Finally, students might also reflect upon any constructive feedback they have received from their peers.

Chapter 11

Directing & Producing

S P E C I A L I Z A T I O N

Overview

This chapter presents the responsibilities of directors and producers in specialized theatrical productions: in Reader's Theatre,
choosing and scripting the text, casting, rehearsing, maintaining
focus, and determining technical elements; in musicals, working
with a music director, choreographer, and technicians to develop
the production concept; in film and TV, working through development, preproduction, production, and postproduction; and in
multimedia and performance art productions, integrating traditional theatrical techniques with technology.

Activities at the end of the chapter allow students to develop
skills in directing and producing specialized forms of theatre, film
and TV, and multimedia and performance art productions.

Objectives

- The student will be able to demonstrate an understanding of
  Reader's Theatre, including script selection and adaptation,
  casting, and production.
- The student will be able to demonstrate an understanding of
  the special considerations required for directing a musical,
  including aspects of selecting a script, developing a concept,
  scheduling, casting, rehearsing, collaborating, and closing the
  production.
- The student will be able to demonstrate an understanding of
  the basic process of directing and producing for film, TV, and
  multimedia productions.
- The student will understand that performance art is an experi-
  mental genre that has few rules and no standard structure.
- The student will be able to use and define appropriate
  theatre/multimedia vocabulary.

Resources

- Performance space
- Videotapes of musicals or TV shows

THE LANGUAGE OF THEATRE

book
final cut
fine cut
footage
location
lot
lyricist
music director
option
rough cut
rushes or **dailies**
soundstage
storyboard
teleplay

- Videocamera and blank videotape
- Scale model of classroom or theatre space
- Information on theatre permissions
- BLM 6 Job Shadow Agreement
- BLM 113 Chapter 11 Test: Directing & Producing
- BLM 126 Section 4 Answer Key
- BLM 137 Alternative Assessment Rubric: Project 35
- BLMs 139, 140 Student Self-Assessment
- OVH 25 Visual Arts Link: Chapter 11 Directing & Producing

There are many additional resources included in the *Teacher's Resource Book*. For those that relate to this chapter, see the chart at the front of this *Teacher's Manual* (pp. xviii–xxi).

Customizing

At-Risk Students

Emphasize that both directing and producing demand "people" skills—the ability to communicate ideas, to persuade others to support your point of view, to create an ensemble, and to critique in a positive way. As a class, discuss how these people skills can also be applied to careers outside the realm of theatre, such as in teaching or in sales.

Classrooms with Limited Resources

With the permission of the administration, have directing students use corridors for rehearsal areas. Other rehearsal space options could include the orchestra pit or the costume and makeup rooms.

Visual Arts Link

Using OVH 25, with *Le Moulin de la Galette* by Pierre-Auguste Renoir, have students imagine that this painting depicts a scene from a musical production. Working in groups of three, with one student acting as director, one as choreographer, and one as music director, have them discuss rehearsal arrangements for this scene. They should look closely at the painting to determine what kinds of activities are going on in the scene, who might be the principals, who might be the secondary characters or chorus, and who might be singing or playing music in the scene. Each group should determine how they must work together as a directing team to coach the actors and musicians in the scene. Have groups present their plans for the rehearsal of this scene.

Side-Coaching Tips

Choosing the Right Work

Directors looking for a suitable Reader's Theatre script often read dozens of literary works. Sometimes what appeals to the eye will not appeal to the ear. Suggest that students read aloud any text they are considering to determine if it sounds as good as it looks.

Children's Reader's Theatre

Small children love the immediacy of live performance. Encourage students to examine children's literature to find a suitable script for a children's Reader's Theatre production. If possible, they might develop and then present their script at a local elementary school.

Gesturing Symbolically

A gesture in a Reader's Theatre production need not be realistic. Tell students that if the script requires one character to give something to another character, Character A can simply extend his or her script toward the audience and Character B can reach toward the audience and pantomime pulling it in. An audience will have no trouble accepting this stylized movement.

Reviewing a Royalty Contract

Help students understand the cost of producing a musical by bringing to class a royalty contract. If possible, have students compare the fees for several different shows and then estimate what a two- or four-performance run would cost.

Staging the Chorus

One of the greatest challenges in directing a musical is staging the chorus. Directing students should work with each chorus member to establish a specific name, occupation, and reason for being there. For blocking purposes, directing students could combine small groups of chorus members into families, business associates, friends, enemies, and so on.

Assessing Blocking

Encourage directing students to see as many musical productions as possible and to analyze the director's blocking of both musical and nonmusical scenes. Have them record particularly striking examples in their Theatre Notebooks.

Following the Leader

If you or some other teacher at your school is directing a musical, encourage interested students to become assistant directors, assistant music directors, or assistant choreographers.

Examining the Power of Posters

Since a poster should reflect the director's production concept, directors and producers should collaborate with the artist in designing a theatre poster. To get the idea of how a poster expresses a production concept, encourage students to examine the design and content of a movie poster both before and after they see the movie it advertises. In their Theatre Notebooks, students should react to the effectiveness of the poster.

Using Technology

Because multimedia performances rely on technology, they are prone to technical difficulties. Remind students who are using technical equipment to do several tech runs before the performance and to have troubleshooting strategies worked out.

Support for Activities

The activities may be used as in-class activities, homework assignments, or as opportunities for extra-credit work. Most can be completed within a week. The Job Shadow—TV Director or Producer activity may continue through the semester or year. Be sure to review with students the guidelines for job shadowing on BLM 6.

Student Assessment

Assessment may be accomplished by measuring achievement of the objectives outlined at the beginning of this lesson plan. Students may demonstrate their success at meeting those objectives through participation in class discussion and fulfillment of assigned activities. You may wish to create your own rubric for assessment. See pages xxii–xxvi for guidance on creating rubrics. A chapter test (BLM 113) may also be used. Project 35: Directing a Reader's Theatre Piece may be used as an alternative, performance-based assessment. (BLM 137 provides a rubric for assessing student performance on this project.)

Self- and group-assessment may take the form of journaling entries in the students' Theatre Notebooks, some of which are part of the chapter activities. Other entries could address self-assessment questions (BLMs 139, 140). Finally, students might also reflect upon any constructive feedback they have received from their peers.

Wilson

SPECIALIZATION

Overview

The historical profile summarizes Wilson's personal and professional life and notes his chief works; discusses African American playwrights and their contribution to American theatre; and examines Wilson's theatrical style, especially his emphasis on story-telling, his distinctive use of language, his incorporation of music, and his desire to trace through his plays the history of 20th-century African Americans. A scene from Wilson's *Seven Guitars* allows students to analyze elements of the playwright's style, paying close attention to focus, pace, and transitions. The Try It Out and Extension activities emphasize directing.

Objectives

- The student will be able to demonstrate a basic knowledge of the life and works of August Wilson.
- The student will be able to demonstrate a basic knowledge of the development of African American theatre.
- The student will be able to demonstrate through performance an understanding of August Wilson's use of storytelling, music, and universal themes in his plays.
- The student will be able to demonstrate an understanding of basic directing techniques, including focus, pace, and transitions.

Resources

- Space sufficient to rehearse and perform the scene
- Guitar case and guitar
- Dress box containing a dress with a long skirt
- Two bus tickets
- An Outline of Theatre History (student text, pp. 1–15)
- *The Book of Scenes for Aspiring Actors* (or other books of scenes)
- BLM 122 Historical Profile Test: Wilson
- BLM 126 Section 4 Answer Key

- BLMs 139, 140 Student Self-Assessment
- BLMs 155, 156 Research Activities: Modern American Theatre

> There are many additional resources included in the *Teacher's Resource Book*. For those that relate to this historical profile, see the chart at the front of this *Teacher's Manual* (pp. xviii–xxi).

Customizing

Students with Learning Disabilities

If a student has difficulty remembering lines, direct him or her to practice aloud; hearing the words will help the student sense the rhythm of Wilson's language. In addition, suggest that the student make a recording of the scene and play it over and over till the words become a part of their character. If the student is still unable to memorize the part, allow him or her to use the script, marking it with symbols denoting places where eye contact is essential.

Links to Literature/Language Arts

Encourage students to compare Wilson's use of language with that of other playwrights they have read. Are Floyd's long speeches, for example, a variation on a Shakespearean monologue?

Research

Have students who are interested in learning more about modern American theatre do one of the research activities on BLMs 155 and 156.

Side-Coaching Tips

The scene from *Seven Guitars* includes sidenotes—comments and questions—in the margins. The following suggestions also provide ongoing support as students direct or perform the scene:

Singing the Blues

To help actors achieve a wide vocal range in this scene, directing students might have their actors sing some of their parts as if they were blues lyrics. Together they should decide how the lines should be read, for example, which lines deserve greatest projection or a change of pitch or rhythm, to best convey the meaning of the words.

Doing Stage Business

When a script calls for an actor to perform a complicated bit of stage business, such as taking an item out of a box, the action must not be clumsy or take too long. Since it might be difficult to hold a dress box and open it at the same time, directing students might have their actors experiment until they find a smooth, quick way to open the box. For example, Floyd might hand the box to Vera so that she holds it steady while he opens it.

Alternative Activities

The following activities may be used as in-class or homework assignments or as opportunities for extra-credit work:

Using Music

Music can be used seriously to reinforce action, characters, and mood, or ironically to contradict them. Have students choose a play and think of two pieces of music, one serious and one ironic, to use as a scene opener or closer.

Choosing the Right Instrument

In making decisions about the music played to begin or end a scene, a director needs to know the sound quality of different musical instruments. Working with the orchestra or band teacher, students can choose a simple 16-bar song and ask student musicians to record it with different combinations of instruments. They should try to work with at least two string, two wind, and two brass instruments. Students can comment on the effects of each combination of instruments in their Theatre Notebooks.

Direct Another Scene

Students might enjoy directing a scene from another August Wilson play, *Joe Turner's Come and Gone,* found on pages 45–50 of *The Book of Scenes for Aspiring Actors.*

Student Assessment

Assessment may be accomplished by measuring achievement of the objectives outlined at the beginning of this lesson plan. Students may demonstrate their success at meeting those objectives through participation in class discussion and in their role in the performance of the scene from *Seven Guitars.* They may also complete the profile test on BLM 122. You may wish to create your own rubric for assessment. See pages xxii–xxvi for guidance on creating rubrics.

Self-assessment may take the form of journaling entries in the students' Theatre Notebooks. Other entries could address self-assessment questions (BLMs 139, 140). Finally, students might also reflect upon any constructive feedback they have received from their peers.

Chapter 12

Technical Theatre

SPECIALIZATION

Overview

This chapter covers specialized techniques in the various areas in technical theatre, including construction of three-dimensional scenery; the use of papier mâché for props; selection and hanging of curtain and drapery fabrics; techniques for making and using bookcases, plants, paintings, smoke and fire effects, and edible and inedible stage food; the use of projectors and projection screens; sound layering, mixing, and uses of the synthesizer; costume fabrication of armor, headpieces, jewelry and ornaments, footwear, draped costumes, and masks; and three-dimensional makeup effects, as well as beards and moustaches, wigs, and stage blood.

In addition to details describing techniques and methods for achieving specialized effects, this chapter also gives useful tips and safety warnings. Activities give students practice in the various techniques described.

THE LANGUAGE OF THEATRE

ambient light

hot spot

keystoning

life mask

profile

swag

synthesizer

three-dimensional scenery

track

voice-over

Objectives

- The student will be able to demonstrate an understanding and working knowledge of the construction of three-dimensional set pieces, such as trees, rocks, and other sculptural forms.

- The student will be able to demonstrate an understanding and working knowledge of the use of papier-mâché in making stage props.

- The student will be able to demonstrate an understanding and working knowledge of stage fabrics for curtains and draperies.

- The student will be able to demonstrate an understanding and working knowledge of using projections for the stage, including lensless and lens projectors, front- and rear-screen projection, and slide preparation.

- The student will be able to demonstrate an understanding of techniques in sound layering, mixing, and using a synthesizer.

- The student will be able to demonstrate an understanding of techniques in costume construction to produce special articles, including masks, armor, decorative jewelry, and footwear.

- The student will be able to demonstrate an understanding and working knowledge of three-dimensional makeup techniques using nose putty, derma wax, latex, and facial hair.

- The student will be able to use and define appropriate technical theatre vocabulary.

Resources

- Shop spaces, tools, and construction supplies as detailed in chapter
- Lighting system, instruments, and supplies as detailed in chapter
- Sound control and recording equipment as detailed in chapter
- Costume shop, tools, and supplies as detailed in chapter
- Makeup supplies and facilities as detailed in chapter
- BLM 102 Making a Life Mask
- BLM 114 Chapter 12 Test: Technical Theatre
- BLM 126 Section 4 Answer Key
- BLM 138 Alternative Assessment Rubric: Project 40
- BLMs 139, 140 Student Self-Assessment
- OVH 26 Visual Arts Link: Chapter 12 Technical Theatre

> There are many additional resources included in the *Teacher's Resource Book*. For those that relate to this chapter, see the chart at the front of this *Teacher's Manual* (pp. xviii–xxi).

Customizing

Classrooms with Limited Resources

If you have no access to a scene shop, demonstrate the construction of full-scale, three-dimensional objects by using matte or poster board, which can be easily cut, glued, and worked within a classroom situation.

English-Language Learners

Backstage areas can be extremely dangerous places, particularly for students whose English is minimal. Guard against student accidents by posting pictorial danger signs at places where accidents can occur. You might work with an ESL teacher or bilingual aide to ensure that students fully understand all safety rules.

Visual Arts Link

Using OVH 26, with *Woman Walking in an Exotic Forest* by Henri Rousseau, have students imagine that this painting is a set rendering for a play, and it's their job to build this set. Working with partners or in small groups, students can discuss the materials and techniques they will use to build the flowers, trees, tropical foliage and grass, and oranges for this three-dimensional set. Remind students that the woman in the painting has to be able to move in and out of the trees and bushes of this set, so they can't simply reproduce the entire painting on a backdrop. One group member should act as recorder to keep a list of materials and techniques to present to the rest of the class.

Side-Coaching Tips

Considering Function

Students designing three-dimensional objects must take into account whether the object will be functional or merely decorative. For example, a rock or a log that will be sat or stood upon requires construction similar to that of a small platform or a stool.

Bracing and Stiffening Profiles

When adding a profile to a flat, the added plywood piece may create an imbalance in the flat. In such instances, advise students to secure the profile with additional bracing or stiffening.

Handling Papier Mâché

Papier mâché set or hand props are desirable on stage because they are lightweight. Explain to students that when actors need to handle or move a papier mâché object that must appear heavy, such as a log, they will need to use their bodies and facial expressions to convey the weight of the actual object.

Also inform students that papier mâché will wear thin with frequent handling so they should not handle such objects any more than necessary.

Avoiding Anachronisms

Current fabric weaves and designs have not always been available. Paisley, for example, was unknown in the Elizabethan era. In choosing fabrics for set decoration, urge students to do some research before settling on a particular fabric or design.

Useful Food Substitutes

Plays featuring an eating scene usually combine edible and inedible food. Any edible food should be inexpensive and easy to swallow. Suggest to students that applesauce is an excellent stage food that can be colored with food coloring to simulate various types of food. Encourage students to share ideas about other appropriate stage foods, based on stipulations in the chapter.

Period Portraits

If students are to create a portrait for stage use, have them determine an appropriate background for the picture. During the Renaissance, for example, artists used landscapes; during the neoclassical period, classical architectural elements were favored. If students are working with a period play, urge them to examine art books containing portraits from that period.

Avoiding Static

When using reel-to-reel tape recorders for sound tapes, students should avoid "white noise," the sound of the stopping and starting of each sound segment. To do so, the technician can fade down and up—but only if he or she knows the tape well.

Spilling Blood

Warn students that whenever possible, the blood pack should not be taped on the actor too early as physical activity might open it before the required time.

Support for Activities

The activities may be used as in-class activities, homework assignments, or as opportunities for extra-credit work. Most can be completed within a week. If students are creating a life mask, you might provide them with BLM 102.

Student Assessment

Assessment may be accomplished by measuring achievement of the objectives outlined at the beginning of this lesson plan. Students may demonstrate their success at meeting those objectives through participation in class discussion and fulfillment of assigned activities. You may wish to create your own rubric for assessment. See pages xxii–xxvi for guidance on creating rubrics. A chapter test (BLM 114) may also be used. Project 40: Making a Mask may be used as an alternative, performance-based assessment. (BLM 138 provides a rubric for assessing student performance on this project.)

Self- and group-assessment may take the form of journaling entries in the students' Theatre Notebooks, some of which are part of the chapter activities. Other entries could address self-assessment questions (BLMs 139, 140). Finally, students might also reflect upon any constructive feedback they have received from their peers.

Project 31

Using an Accent

SPECIALIZATION

Assignment

Perform a monologue using an accent.

Objectives

- The student will be able to recognize and use regional American and foreign accents to express appropriate characterization.
- The student will be able to identify and utilize various resources to learn and authenticate regional American and foreign accents to express appropriate characterization.

Resources

- Audiotape recorder and blank tape
- BLM 136 Alternative Assessment Rubric: Project 31
- BLMs 139, 140 Student Self-Assessment

> There are many additional resources included in the *Teacher's Resource Book*. For those that relate to this project, see the chart at the front of this *Teacher's Manual* (pp. xviii–xxi).

Creating

Remind students not to memorize lines first and then add the accent. The rhythm and pronunciation will be set and hard to change. The sound of the accent should be in the actor's head as he or she begins to memorize.

Performing

Suggest to students that before the actual performance, they find a line of dialogue that they are confident saying with an accent. They should say it over and over so that the feel and rhythm of the accent carries over to the performance.

Responding

You and the students may assess the projects using a rubric you have created. (See pages xxii–xxvi for guidance on creating rubrics.) Remind students to give each other positive, constructive feedback. Students may also use the prompts on BLMs 139, 140 to do self-assessment. Students may record their reactions to their own and to others' projects in their Theatre Notebooks. This project, which is an alternative assessment for Chapter 10, may also be evaluated by using BLM 136.

Project 32

Performing a Song

S P E C I A L I Z A T I O N

Assignment

Perform a song from a musical.

Objectives

- The student will be able to use and adapt acting skills (characterization, subtext, and so on) for performance in musical theatre.
- The student will be able to demonstrate an ability to utilize the elements (singing, choreography, and so on) of musical theatre in performance.

Resources

- Rehearsal and performance space
- Music
- Tape player (if using taped accompaniment)
- Musical instrument (if using live accompaniment)
- BLMs 139, 140 Student Self-Assessment

There are many additional resources included in the *Teacher's Resource Book*. For those that relate to this project, see the chart at the front of this *Teacher's Manual* (pp. xviii–xxi).

Creating

Stress that blocking during songs needs to be as motivated as it is during spoken dialogue. Just as the character's life continues every moment the actor is onstage in a play, the character's life continues in a musical even when the actor is not singing during a song. Inexperienced actors may make the mistake of acting only when they are singing.

Performing

Singers using recorded accompaniment must work closely with the person handling the tape or CD player so that he or she knows exactly when to start the music; otherwise, the result will be an awkward pause during any transition from spoken to sung lines.

Responding

You and the students may assess the projects using a rubric you have created. (See pages xxii–xxvi for guidance on creating rubrics.) Remind students to give each other positive, constructive feedback. Students may also use the prompts on BLMs 139, 140 to do self-assessment. Students may record their reactions to their own and to others' projects in their Theatre Notebooks.

Project 33

Staging a Fight
SPECIALIZATION

Assignment

With one or two partners, perform a scene with stage combat.

Objectives

- The student will be able to demonstrate an understanding of simple, safe stage combat movement.
- The student will be able to demonstrate ensemble and rehearsal skills.

Resources

- Rehearsal and performance space
- BLMs 139, 140 Student Self-Assessment

There are many additional resources included in the *Teacher's Resource Book.* For those that relate to this project, see the chart at the front of this *Teacher's Manual* (pp. xviii–xxi).

Creating

Remind students that the receiver in a fight scene is in control of the action. This does not mean that the giver may be out of control; rather, it means that the giver must yield if the receiver feels any pain or too much pressure in any movement.

Performing

Suggest to students that exhaled breath or other sounds from both combatants will add realism to the fight. Also, students who are the givers should indicate by some means, such as rubbing their knuckles afterward, that the impact of the blow hurt them as well as the receiver.

Responding

You and the students may assess the projects using a rubric you have created. (See pages xxii–xxvi for guidance on creating rubrics.) Remind students to give each other positive, constructive feedback. Students may also use the prompts on BLMs 139, 140 to do self-assessment. Students may record their reactions to their own and to others' projects in their Theatre Notebooks.

Project 34

Acting On-Camera

S P E C I A L I Z A T I O N

Assignment

With an ensemble, perform a scene from a play to be recorded on videotape.

Objectives

- The student will be able to use and adapt acting skills (characterization, movement, blocking, subtext, and so on) for on-camera performance.
- The student will be able to demonstrate ensemble and rehearsal skills.
- The student will be able to demonstrate an understanding of film and video terminology.

Resources

- Video camera and blank videotape
- Editing equipment (if required)
- Props, costumes, and makeup
- Lighting equipment
- TV monitor
- VCR
- BLMs 139, 140 Student Self-Assessment

There are many additional resources included in the *Teacher's Resource Book*. For those that relate to this project, see the chart at the front of this *Teacher's Manual* (pp. xviii–xxi).

Creating

Remind directors that since filming involves shooting sections of a play, not scenes, frequent stops are the norm. Remind them also to be mindful of focus. In a scene in which Actor A is talking, a listening Actor B can change the focus of the viewers by an eye movement or a slight movement of a finger. Finally, warn directors to test fabrics and colors for their effect on videotape and with the available lighting so that they know which fabrics and colors to avoid. For example, white reflects, shutting down the lens and thus darkening a scene.

Performing

If the action in a scene is stopped and then resumed, it's imperative for each actor or the director to replicate precisely each actor's previous position to maintain continuity. Students may wish to enlist a volunteer to watch for continuity.

Responding

You and the students may assess the projects using a rubric you have created. (See pages xxii–xxvi for guidance on creating rubrics.) Remind students to give each other positive, constructive feedback. Students may also use the prompts on BLMs 139, 140 to do self-assessment. Students may record their reactions to their own and to others' projects in their Theatre Notebooks.

Directing a Reader's Theatre Piece

S P E C I A L I Z A T I O N

Assignment

Direct an ensemble in a Reader's Theatre presentation.

Objectives

- The student will be able to demonstrate an understanding of the unique acting and directing techniques required for Reader's Theatre.
- The student will be able to develop a working script for Reader's Theatre, including identifying the required production elements (sound effect sources, necessary equipment, and so on).

Resources

- Rehearsal space
- Chairs or stools
- Lecterns (if required)
- Script holders
- Audiotape player with recorded sound (if required)
- BLM 137 Alternative Assessment Rubric: Project 35
- BLMs 139, 140 Student Self-Assessment

> There are many additional resources included in the *Teacher's Resource Book*. For those that relate to this project, see the chart at the front of this *Teacher's Manual* (pp. xviii–xxi).

Creating

During early rehearsals directing students should experiment with different presentation styles—no movement except gestures; full movement; no interaction; stylized movement—to determine which is most suitable for the script and the ensemble. They should record an early rehearsal so that the ensemble can hear vocal nuances (or the lack of them).

Performing

For a uniform effect, the actors should hold their scripts similarly—folded over, full open, waist high. Even more important, they should never let the script cover their faces from any angle or sight line in the audience. Placing scripts on music stands, set at chest height, is an option.

Responding

You and the students may assess the projects using a rubric you have created. (See pages xxii–xxvi for guidance on creating rubrics.) Remind students to give each other positive, constructive feedback. Students may also use the prompts on BLMs 139, 140 to do self-assessment. Students may record their reactions to their own and to others' projects in their Theatre Notebooks. This project, which is an alternative assessment for Chapter 11, may also be evaluated by using BLM 137.

Project 36

Developing a Musical
SPECIALIZATION

Assignment

With a group, develop a musical based on a short story or non-musical play.

Objectives

- The student will be able to demonstrate an understanding of the importance of collaboration in musical theatre.
- The student will be able to demonstrate an understanding of the unique considerations required for writing material for musical theatre.

Resources

- Music paper
- Music and blocking rehearsal space
- Recorded music or live instruments

- Appropriate sets, props, lighting, sound, costumes, and makeup
- BLMs 139, 140 Student Self-Assessment

> There are many additional resources included in the *Teacher's Resource Book*. For those that relate to this project, see the chart at the front of this *Teacher's Manual* (pp. xviii–xxi).

Creating

Remind students that this is a collaborative effort. Reaching a consensus on the material to be adapted is very important for all of the group; each member should have "ownership" in developing the project. Encourage students to do research by listening to or watching a selection of musicals to become more familiar with the genre.

Performing

Encourage students to rehearse with as many of the technical aspects as they can and as much as possible before the performance. Musicals are heavily dependent on coordinated teamwork. Students should try to anticipate any problems before they occur.

Responding

You and the students may assess the projects using a rubric you have created. (See pages xxii–xxvi for guidance on creating rubrics.) Remind students to give each other positive, constructive feedback. Students may also use the prompts on BLMs 139, 140 to do self-assessment. Students may record their reactions to their own and to others' projects in their Theatre Notebooks.

Project 37

Three-Dimensional Scenery

Assignment

Alone or with a partner, construct a three-dimensional set piece of a rock or log.

Objectives

- The student will be able to demonstrate an understanding of measurement and scale to draw a rendering of a three-dimensional set piece.
- The student will be able to demonstrate an understanding of basic set construction by building and finishing (painting) a three-dimensional set piece.

Resources

- Paper, lead and colored pencils, ruler
- Plywood, lumber, chicken wire
- Saw, hammer, nails, trimmers (wire cutters)
- Appropriate covering materials
- Paint brushes
- White latex paint for sizing
- Finishing paint in appropriate colors
- BLMs 139, 140 Student Self-Assessment

> There are many additional resources included in the *Teacher's Resource Book*. For those that relate to this project, see the chart at the front of this *Teacher's Manual* (pp. xviii–xxi).

Creating

Suggest that students review the painting techniques on pages 223–225 of the student text for painting rocks or log surfaces. Remind students to use 3/4-inch plywood if actors must sit or stand on the rocks or logs.

Presenting

For ease in carrying a large log or a standing tree stump during scene shifts, cut a handhold in the flat, top part; grabbing the stump by any parts covered by chicken wire ultimately damages the surface.

Responding

You and the students may assess the projects using a rubric you have created. (See pages xxii–xxvi for guidance on creating rubrics.) Remind students to give each other positive, constructive feedback. Students may also use the prompts on BLMs 139, 140 to do self-assessment. Students may record their reactions to their own and to others' projects in their Theatre Notebooks.

Projecting a Background

S P E C I A L I Z A T I O N

Assignment

Alone or with a partner, create two slides for projected scenery.

Objectives

- The student will be able to demonstrate an understanding of developing and creating projections for the stage.
- The student will be able to demonstrate the ability to utilize research skills in selecting images for projections for the stage.

Resources

- Lensless or lens projector
- Projection screen
- Glass for ink painting
- Projection-grade glass to protect the slides
- Transparent inks, dark construction paper, or photographic transparencies (as required)
- BLMs 139, 140 Student Self-Assessment

> There are many additional resources included in the *Teacher's Resource Book*. For those that relate to this project, see the chart at the front of this *Teacher's Manual* (pp. xviii–xxi).

Creating

Suggest to students that projection limitations make a realistic background difficult to accomplish; thus, stylized backgrounds are more practical in establishing an appropriate mood. If the screen used for rear-screen projections needs cleaning, students should use a commercial product that will clean without damaging the screen or leaving streaks. To avoid blank spaces at the top, bottom, or sides, students should check proportions of projection to surface.

Presenting

If a production calls for multiple slides or projections to directly follow one another, recommend that students use two projectors; then, rather than "clicking" on and off at each slide change, one image can fade out as another fades in.

Responding

You and the students may assess the projects using a rubric you have created. (See pages xxii–xxvi for guidance on creating rubrics.) Remind students to give each other positive, constructive feedback. Students may also use the prompts on BLMs 139, 140 to do self-assessment. Students may record their reactions to their own and to others' projects in their Theatre Notebooks.

Project 39

Creating Jewelry

S P E C I A L I Z A T I O N

Assignment

Create a piece of stage jewelry.

Objectives

- The student will be able to demonstrate an understanding of basic jewelry construction.
- The student will be able to demonstrate research skills in selecting designs, patterns, and character appropriateness for jewelry.

Resources

- Papier mâché, sized felt, foam rubber, or wood
- White glue and hot-glue gun
- Paint (if desired)
- Glass or plastic "jewels," beads, or other decorative items
- Padding, combs, or chains (if needed)
- BLMs 139, 140 Student Self-Assessment

There are many additional resources included in the *Teacher's Resource Book*. For those that relate to this project, see the chart at the front of this *Teacher's Manual* (pp. xviii–xxi).

Creating

Encourage students to take a trip to a hobby shop or craft shop and to a hardware store. They should walk down each aisle taking notes on the variety of potential raw materials available for making jewelry. Seeing a particular item may give them inspiration as to what kind of jewelry they would like to make and how they might make it.

Presenting

Due to the fragile nature of many jewelry items, students should devise a system for storing and handling the jewelry whenever it's not being worn. If space is available, a prop table for the jewelry could be designated, the costume crew could collect and store the jewelry, or an area in the dressing room could be set aside for the jewelry of each actor. Suggest hooks for hanging necklaces to keep them from getting tangled and cups for holding rings and earrings so they don't get lost.

Responding

You and the students may assess the projects using a rubric you have created. (See pages xxii–xxvi for guidance on creating rubrics.) Remind students to give each other positive, constructive feedback. Students may also use the prompts on BLMs 139, 140 to do self-assessment. Students may record their reactions to their own and to others' projects in their Theatre Notebooks.

Project 40

Making a Mask

S P E C I A L I Z A T I O N

Assignment

Create a mask for a specific character in a play or one that can be used in a variety of theatre productions.

Objectives

- The student will be able to demonstrate an understanding of basic mask-construction techniques.
- The student will be able to demonstrate research skills in selecting appropriate designs for mask construction.

Resources

- Sketching materials
- Actor or wig stand
- Basic mask materials as detailed in project
- Petroleum jelly
- Paper towels
- Sandpaper
- Paint
- Beard and wig materials (if desired)
- Liner fabric and/or cushioning material
- Elastic or ribbon ties (if needed)
- BLM 138 Alternative Assessment Rubric: Project 40
- BLMs 139, 140 Student Self-Assessment

There are many additional resources included in the *Teacher's Resource Book*. For those that relate to this project, see the chart at the front of this *Teacher's Manual* (pp. xviii–xxi).

Creating

Warn students that wig stands are usually made of styrofoam and are not very stable. To avoid having them fall over during mask construction, students should affix the wig stands to a sturdy base using glue or sticky putty.

Presenting

To ensure a smooth presentation, students should work with their masks ahead of time, practicing modeling the mask in different positions and in different lighting conditions.

Responding

You and the students may assess the projects using a rubric you have created. (See pages xxii–xxvi for guidance on creating rubrics.) Remind students to give each other positive, constructive feedback. Students may also use the prompts on BLMs 139, 140 to do self-assessment. Students may record their reactions to their own and to others' projects in their Theatre Notebooks. This project, which is an alternative assessment for Chapter 12, may also be evaluated by using BLM 138.

Resources

For additional material on specific subjects, consult the following books:

Acting

Adler, Stella. *The Technique of Acting.* New York: Bantam, 1990.

Alberts, David. *Talking About Mime.* Portsmouth, NH: Heinemann, 1994.

——. *The Expressive Body; Physical Characterization for the Actor.* Portsmouth, NH: Heinemann, 1997.

Barton, John. *Playing Shakespeare.* New York: Methuen, 1985.

Barton, Robert. *Acting Onstage and Off.* New York: Harcourt Brace, 1993.

——. *Style for Actors.* Mountain View, CA: Mayfield Publishing Co., 1993.

Belt, Lynda. *Improv Game Book II: A Source Book for Improvisation Performance Training and Games.* Puyallup, WA: Thespis Productions, 1994.

Belt, Lynda, and Rebecca Stockley. *Improvisation Through Theatre Sports.* Seattle, WA: Thespis Productions, 1991.

Benedetti, Robert L. *The Actor at Work.* 7th ed. Boston: Allyn & Bacon, 1996.

Boleslavsky, Richard. *Acting: The First Six Lessons.* New York: Routledge, 1987.

Chekhov, Michael. *On the Technique of Acting: The First Complete Edition of Chekhov's Classic to the Actor.* New York: HarperCollins, 1993.

Cohen, Robert. *Acting One,* 3rd ed. Mountain View, CA: Mayfield Publishing Co., 1998.

——. *Acting Professionally: Raw Facts about Careers in Acting.* Mountain View, CA: Mayfield Publishing Co., 1997.

Downs, David. *The Actor's Eye: Seeing and Being Seen.* Applause Books, New York: 1995.

Felnagle, Richard H. *Beginning Acting.* Englewood Cliffs, NJ: Prentice-Hall, 1987.

Hagen, Uta. *A Challenge for the Actor.* New York: Scribner's, 1991.

——. *Respect for Acting.* New York: Macmillan, 1979.

Hooks, Ed. *The Ultimate Scene and Monologue Sourcebook.* New York: Back Stage Books, 1994.

McGaw, Charles J., and Larry D. Clark. *Acting Is Believing.* New York: Harcourt Brace, 1992.

O'Neill, Rosary. *The Actor's Checklist*. New York: Harcourt Brace, 1992.

Perry, John. *Encyclopedia of Acting Techniques*. Cincinnati, OH: Betterway Books, 1997.

Richards, Thomas, and Jerzy Grotowski. *At Work with Grotowski on Physical Actions*. New York: Routledge, 1995.

Sabatine, Jean. *Movement Training for the Stage and Screen*. New York: Back Stage Books, 1995.

Stanislavski, Constantin. *An Actor Prepares*. Trans. by Elizabeth Reynolds Hapgood. New York: Theatre Arts Books, 1989.

——. *Building a Character*. Trans. by Elizabeth Reynolds Hapgood. New York: Theatre Arts Books, 1989.

——. *Creating a Role*. Trans. by Elizabeth Reynolds Hapgood. New York: Theatre Arts Books, 1989.

White, Edward, and Marguerite Rattye. *Acting and Stage Movement*. Boston: Baker's Plays, 1990.

Careers

Ball, Victoria K. *Opportunities in Interior Design and Decorating Careers*. Lincolnwood, IL: VGM Career Horizons, 1995.

Bekken, Bonnie Bjorguine. *Opportunities in Performing Arts Careers*. Lincolnwood, IL: VGM Career Horizons, 1991.

Bly, Robert W. *Careers for Writers & Others Who Have a Way with Words*. Lincolnwood, IL: VGM Career Horizons, 1996.

Bone, Jan. *Opportunities in Cable Television Careers*. Lincolnwood, IL: VGM Career Horizons, 1993.

——. *Opportunities in Film Careers*. Lincolnwood, IL: VGM Career Horizons, 1990.

Brescoll, James, and Ralph Dahm. *Opportunities in Sales Careers*. Lincolnwood, IL: VGM Career Horizons, 1995.

Camenson, Blythe. *Careers for Self-Starters & Other Entrepreneurial Types*. Lincolnwood, IL: VGM Career Horizons, 1997.

——. *Great Jobs for Art Majors*. Lincolnwood, IL: VGM Career Horizons, 1997.

——. *Great Jobs for Communications Majors*. Lincolnwood, IL: VGM Career Horizons, 1995.

——. *Great Jobs for Liberal Arts Majors*. Lincolnwood, IL: VGM Career Horizons, 1997.

——. *Opportunities in Museum Careers*. Lincolnwood, IL: VGM Career Horizons, 1996.

——. *Real People Working in Education*. Lincolnwood, IL: VGM Career Horizons, 1997.

——. *Real People Working in Sales & Marketing*. Lincolnwood, IL: VGM Career Horizons, 1997.

——. *VGM's Career Portraits: Writing*. Lincolnwood, IL: VGM Career Horizons, 1996.

Chirico, JoAnn. *VGM's Career Portraits: Electronics.* Lincolnwood, IL: VGM Career Portraits, 1996.

DeGalan, Julie, and Stephen Lambert. *Great Jobs for English Majors.* Lincolnwood, IL: VGM Career Horizons, 1994.

Dolber, Roslyn. *Opportunities in Fashion Careers.* Lincolnwood, IL: VGM Career Horizons, 1993.

Eberts, Marjorie, Margaret Gisler, and Maria Gisler. *Careers for High-Energy People & Other Go-Getters.* Lincolnwood, IL: VGM Career Horizons, 1998.

Eberts, Marjorie, and Margaret Gisler. *VGM's Career Portraits: Teaching.* Lincolnwood, IL: VGM Career Horizons, 1995.

Edelfelt, Roy A. *Careers in Education.* Lincolnwood, IL: VGM Career Horizons, 1998.

Ellis, Elmo I. *Opportunities in Broadcasting Careers.* Lincolnwood, IL: VGM Career Horizons, 1992.

Foote-Smith, Elizabeth. *Opportunities in Writing Careers.* Lincolnwood, IL: VGM Career Horizons, 1989.

Garner, Geraldine O. *Careers in Social and Rehabilitation Services.* Lincolnwood, IL: VGM Career Horizons, 1994.

Gearhart, Susan Wood. *Opportunities in Beauty Culture Careers.* Lincolnwood, IL: VGM Career Horizons, 1996.

——. *Opportunities in Modeling Careers.* Lincolnwood, IL: VGM Career Horizons, 1991.

Gerardi, Robert. *Opportunities in Music Careers.* Lincolnwood, IL: VGM Career Horizons, 1997.

Gisler, Maria. *VGM's Career Portraits: Art.* Lincolnwood, IL: VGM Career Horizons, 1998.

Goldberg, Jan. *Careers for Courageous People & Other Adventurous Types.* Lincolnwood, IL: VGM Career Horizons, 1998.

——. *Great Jobs for Music Majors.* Lincolnwood, IL: VGM Career Horizons, 1998.

——. *Great Jobs for Theater Majors.* Lincolnwood, IL: VGM Career Horizons, 1998.

——. *Real People Working in Communications.* Lincolnwood, IL: VGM Career Horizons, 1997.

Gordon, Barbara. *Opportunities in Commercial Art and Graphic Design Careers.* Lincolnwood, IL: VGM Career Horizons, 1998.

Greenspon, Jaq. *Careers for Film Buffs & Other Hollywood Types.* Lincolnwood, IL: VGM Career Horizons, 1993.

——. *VGM's Career Portraits: Acting.* Lincolnwood, IL: VGM Career Horizons, 1996.

——. *VGM's Career Portraits: Music.* Lincolnwood, IL: VGM Career Horizons, 1995.

Johnson, Jeff. *Careers for Music Lovers & Other Tuneful Types.* Lincolnwood, IL: VGM Career Horizons, 1997.

Lambert, Stephen. *Great Jobs for Business Majors.* Lincolnwood, IL: VGM Career Horizons, 1996.

Marek, Rosanne J. *Opportunities in Social Science Careers.* Lincolnwood, IL: VGM Career Horizons, 1997.

Mauro, Lucia. *Careers for Fashion Plates & Other Trendsetters.* Lincolnwood, IL: VGM Career Horizons, 1996.

——. *Careers for the Stagestruck & Other Dramatic Types.* Lincolnwood, IL: VGM Career Horizons, 1997.

——. *VGM's Career Portraits: Fashion.* Lincolnwood, IL: VGM Career Horizons, 1996.

Moore, Dick. *Opportunities in Acting Careers.* Lincolnwood, IL: VGM Career Horizons, 1993.

Munday, Marianne F. *Opportunities in Crafts Careers.* Lincolnwood, IL: VGM Career Horizons, 1994.

Nelson, John Oliver. *Opportunities in Religious Service Careers.* Lincolnwood, IL: VGM Career Horizons, 1988.

Noronha, Shonan F.R. *Careers in Communications.* Lincolnwood, IL: VGM Career Horizons, 1994.

——. *Opportunities in Television and Video Careers.* 1994.

Pattis, S. William, and Robert A. Carter. *Opportunities in Publishing Careers.* Lincolnwood, IL: VGM Career Horizons, 1995.

Piper, Robert. *Opportunities in Architectural Careers.* Lincolnwood, IL: VGM Career Horizons, 1993.

Place, Irene. *Opportunities in Business Management Careers.* Lincolnwood, IL: VGM Career Horizons, 1998.

Ring, Trudy. *Careers in Finance.* Lincolnwood, IL: VGM Career Horizons, 1993.

Rotman, Morris B. *Opportunities in Public Relations Careers.* Lincolnwood, IL: VGM Career Horizons, 1995.

Rowh, Mark. *Careers for Crafty People & Other Dexterous Types.* Lincolnwood, IL: VGM Career Horizons, 1994.

——. *Opportunities in Drafting Careers.* Lincolnwood, IL: VGM Career Horizons, 1994.

——. *VGM's Career Portraits: Crafts.* Lincolnwood, IL: VGM Career Horizons, 1996.

Salmon, Mark. *Opportunities in Visual Arts Careers.* Lincolnwood, IL: VGM Career Horizons, 1993.

Stair, Lila B. *Careers in Marketing.* Lincolnwood, IL: VGM Career Horizons, 1995.

Steinberg, Margery. *Opportunities in Marketing Careers,* Lincolnwood, IL: VGM Career Horizons, 1994.

Sumichrast, Michael. *Opportunities in Building Construction Trades,* Lincolnwood, IL: VGM Career Horizons, 1989.

——. *Opportunities in Financial Careers,* Lincolnwood, IL: VGM Career Horizons, 1998.

Weeks, Zona R. *Opportunities in Occupational Therapy Careers,* Lincolnwood, IL: VGM Career Horizons, 1995.

Wood, Robert. *Opportunities in Electrical Trades,* Lincolnwood, IL: VGM Career Horizons, 1997.

Costumes

Boucher, François. *Twenty-Thousand Years of Fashion: The History of Costume and Personal Adornment.* New York: Abrams, 1987.

Holkeboer, Katherine Brand. *Patterns for Theatrical Costumes: Garments, Trims, and Accessories form Ancient Egypt to 1915.* New York: Drama Publishers, 1993.

Kidd, Mary T. *Stage Costume Step-by-Step.* Cincinnati, OH: Betterway Books, 1996.

Laver, James, and Amy De La Haep. *Costumes and Fashion: A Concise History.* New York: Thames and Hudson, 1995.

Motley. *Designing and Making Stage Costumes.* New York: Theatre Arts Books, 1995.

O'Daniel, Georgia. *A Handbook of Costume Drawing.* Stoneham, MA: Focal Press, 1992.

Waugh, Norah. *The Cut of Men's Clothes 1600–1900.* New York: Theatre Arts Books, 1994.

——. *The Cut of Women's Clothes 1600–1930.* New York: Theatre Arts Books, 1994.

Directing

Alberts, David. *Rehearsal Management for Directors.* Portsmouth, NH: Heinemann, 1995.

Bartow, Arthur. *The Director's Voice: Twenty-one Interviews.* New York: Theatre Communications Group, 1989.

Clurman, Harold. *On Directing.* New York: Macmillan, 1997.

Cole, Toby, and Helen K. Chinoy, eds. *Directors on Directing.* New York: Macmillan, 1990.

Converse, Terry John. *Directing for the Stage.* Greenville, GA: Meriwether Publishers, Inc., 1995.

Dean, Alexander, and Lawrence Carra. *Fundamentals of Play Directing.* New York: Holt, Rinehart and Winston, 1988.

Frerer, Lloyd Anton. *Directing for the Stage.* Lincolnwood, IL: National Textbook Co., 1996.

Grote, David. *Play Directing in the School.* Greenville, GA: Meriwether Publishers, Inc., 1997.

——. *Script Analysis: Reading and Understanding the Playscript for Production.* Belmont, CA: Wadsworth, 1985.

Hodge, Francis. *Play Directing: Analysis, Communication, and Style.* Englewood Cliffs, NJ: Prentice-Hall, 1994.

Johnstone, Keith. *Impro: Improvisation and the Theatre.* New York: Theatre Arts Books, 1989.

Rodgers, James W. *Play Director's Survival Kit: A Complete Step-by-step Guide to Producing Theatre in Any School or Community Setting.* Englewood Cliffs, NJ: Prentice-Hall, 1997.

Spolin, Viola. *Theatre Games for Rehearsal: A Director's Handbook.* Evanston, IL: Northwestern University Press, 1987.

Taylor, Don. *Directing Plays.* New York: Theatre Arts Books, 1997.

Thomas, James. *Script Analysis for Actors, Directors and Designers.* Stoneham, MA: Focal Press, 1992.

Lighting

Boulanger, Norman C., and Warren C. Lounsbury. *Theatre Lighting from A to Z.* Seattle: University of Washington Press, 1992.

Cunningham, Glen. *Stage Lighting Revealed: A Design and Execution Handbook.* Cincinnati, OH: Betterway Books, 1993.

Essig, Linda. *Lighting and the Design Idea.* Fort Worth, TX: Harcourt Brace College Publishers, 1996.

Fraser, Neil. *Lighting and Sound.* San Francisco: Phaidon/Chronicle Books, 1995.

Gillette, J. Michael. *Designing with Light.* Mountain View, CA: Mayfield Publishing Co., 1997.

Palmer, Richard H. *The Lighting Art.* Englewood Cliffs, NJ: Prentice-Hall, 1994.

Parker, W. Oren. *Scene Design and Stage Lighting.* Fort Worth, TX: Harcourt, Brace College Publishers, 1996.

Pilbrow, Richard. *Stage Lighting.* New York: Drama Publishers, 1991.

Pilbrow, Richard, and Harold Prince. *Stage Lighting Design: The Art, the Craft, the Life.* New York: Drama Publishers, 1997.

Reid, Francis. *ABC of Stage Lighting.* New York: Drama Publishers, 1992.

Sweet, Harvey. *Handbook of Scenery, Properties, and Lighting: Lighting Volume 2.* Boston: Allyn and Bacon, 1995.

Makeup

Baird, John. *Makeup.* Boston: Baker's Plays, 1990.

Baker, Patsy. *Wigs and Makeup for Theatre, TV and Film.* Stoneham, MA: Focal Press, 1992.

Corey, Irene. *The Mask of Reality: An Approach to Design for the Theatre.* Anchorage, KY: Anchorage Press, 1968.

Corson, Richard. *Fashions in Hair: The First Five Thousand Years.* London: Peter Owen, 1971.

—. *Stage Makeup.* Englewood Cliffs, NJ: Prentice-Hall, 1989.

Holt, Michael. *Costume and Makeup.* New York: Shirmer Books, 1989.

Knapp, Jack Stuart. *The Technique of Stage Makeup.* Boston: Baker's Plays, 1990.

Swinfield, Rosemarie. *Stage Makeup Step-by-Step.* Cincinnati, OH: Betterway Books, 1995.

Musical Theatre

Alper, Steve M. *Next: Auditioning for the Musical Theatre*. Illustrated by Herbert Knapp. Portsmouth, NH: Heinemann, 1997.

Block, Geoffrey, and Fred L. Block. *Enchanted Evenings: The Broadway Musical from Show Boat to Sondheim*. New York: Oxford University Press, 1997.

Bloom, Ken. *American Song: The Complete Musical Theatre Companion 1877–1995*. New York: Macmillan Library Reference, 1996.

Boland, Robert, and Paul Argentini. *Musicals! Directing School and Community Theatre*. Lanham, MD: Scarecrow Press, 1997.

Ganzl, Kurt. *Encyclopedia of the Musical Theatre*. New York: Macmillan Library Reference, 1994.

Horn, Barbara Lee. *The Age of Hair: Evolution and Impact of Broadway's First Rock Musical*. New York: Greenwood Publishing Group, 1991.

Jones, Tom. *Making Musicals: An Informal Introduction to the World of Musical Theatre*. New York: Limelight Editions, 1998.

Miller, Scott. *From Assassins to West Side Story: The Director's Guide to Musical Theatre*. Portsmouth, NH: Heinemann, 1996.

Novak, Deborah, and Elaine Adams Novak. *Staging Musical Theatre*. Cincinnati, OH: Betterway Books, 1996.

Novak, Elaine Adams. *Performing in Musicals*. New York: Shirmer Books, 1988.

Young, David. *How to Direct a Musical: Broadway—Your Way!* New York: Routledge, 1995.

Props

Beck, Roy A. *Stagecraft*. Lincolnwood, IL: National Textbook Co., 1990.

Carnaby, Ann J. *A Guidebook for Creating Three-Dimensional Theatre Art*. Portsmouth, NH: Heinemann, 1997.

Govier, Jacquie. *Create Your Own Stage Props*. Englewood Cliffs, NJ: Prentice-Hall, 1986.

Holt, Michael. *Stage Design and Properties*. San Francisco: Phaidon/Chronicle Books, 1995.

James, Thurston. *The Theatre Props Handbook*. Cincinnati, OH: Betterway Books, 1987.

Lord, Warren. *Stagecraft I*. Woodstock, IL: The Dramatic Publishing Co., 1990.

Motley. *Theatre Props*. New York: DBS Publications, 1977.

Sweet, Harvey. *Handbook of Scenery, Properties, and Lighting: Scenery and Props Volume 1*. Englewood Cliffs, NJ: Prentice-Hall, 1994.

Set Design and Construction

Arnold, Richard L. *Scene Technology*. 3rd ed. Englewood Cliffs, NJ: Prentice-Hall, 1994.

Gillette, J. Michael. *Theatrical Design and Production*. Mountain View, CA: Mayfield Publishing Company, 1996.

Glerum, Jay O. *Stage Rigging Handbook*. 2nd ed. Carbondale, IL: Southern Illinois University Press, 1997.

Lord, William H. *Stagecraft I: A Complete Guide to Backstage Work*. Greenville, GA: Meriwether Publishers, Inc., 1991.

Parker, W. Oren. *Scene Design and Stage Lighting*. Fort Worth, TX: Harcourt, Brace College Publishers, 1996.

Pecktal, Lynn. *Designing and Drawing for the Theatre*. New York: McGraw-Hill, 1995.

Raoul, Bill. *Stock Scenery Construction Handbook*. New York: Broadway Press, 1990.

Reid, Francis. *Designing for the Theatre*. New York: Theatre Arts Books, 1989.

——. *The ABC of Stage Technology*. Portsmouth, NH: Heinemann, 1995.

Rose, Rich. *Drawing Scenery for Theatre, Film, and Television*. Cincinnati, OH: Betterway Books, 1994.

Smith, Ron and Lee, Ming Cho. *American Set Design Two*. New York: Theatre Communications Group, 1991.

Sound

Collison, David. *Stage Sound*. New York: Drama Book Publishers, 1982.

Finelli, Patrick M. *Sound for the Stage*. Boston: Baker's Plays, 1990.

Fraser, Neil. *Lighting and Sound*. San Francisco: Phaidon/Chronicle Books, 1995.

Streader, Timothy, and John Williams. *Create Your Own Stage Lighting*. Englewood Cliffs, NJ: Prentice-Hall, 1986.

Walne, Graham, and Joe Aveline. *Effects for the Theatre*. New York: Drama Publishers, 1995.

Theatre History

Barranger, Milly S. *Theatre: A Way of Seeing*. Belmont, CA: Wadsworth Publishing, 1994.

Bate, Johnathan. *Shakespeare: An Illustrated Stage History*. New York: Oxford University Press, 1996.

Brockett, Oscar G. *History of the Theatre*. Boston: Allyn & Bacon, 1995.

Brockett, Oscar G., and Robert Findlay. *Century of Innovation: A History of European and American Theatre and Drama Since the Late Nineteenth Century*. Boston: Allyn & Bacon, 1991.

Brown, Gene. *Show Time: A Chronology of Broadway and the Theatre from its Beginnings to the Present.* New York: Macmillan General Reference, 1998.

Brown, John Russell, ed. *The Oxford Illustrated History of Theatre.* New York: Oxford University Press, 1997.

Day, Barry. *This Wooden O: Shakespeare's Globe Reborn.* New York: Limelight Editions, 1998.

Green, J. R. *Images of the Greek Theatre.* Austin: University of Texas Press, 1995.

Hischak, Thomas S. *The Theatregoer's Almanac: A Collection of Lists, People, History, and Commentary on the American Theatre.* New York: Greenwood Publishing Group, 1997.

Wilmeth, Don B., ed. *The Cambridge History of American Theatre: Beginning to Post-Civil War.* New York: Cambridge University Press, 1998.

Wise, Jennifer. *Dionysus Writes: The Invention of Theatre in Ancient Greece.* Ithaca, NY: Cornell University Press, 1998.

Theatre Management and Publicity

Byrnes, William J. *Management and the Arts.* Stoneham, MA: Focal Press, 1993.

Chartier, George E. *Full House: The Definitive Guide for Successfully Promoting School and Community Theatre.* Mansfield Center, CT: Dramatic Concepts Publishers, 1992.

Farber, Donald C. *From Option to Opening: A Guide to Producing Plays Off-Broadway.* New York: Limelight Editions, 1989.

Langley, Stephen. *Theatre Management in America.* New York: Drama Publishers, 1995.

McArthur, Nancy. *How to Do Theatre Publicity.* Berea, OH: Good Ideas Co., 1978.

Stern, Lawrence. *Stage Management.* Boston: Allyn & Bacon, 1997.

Resources

The following list is current at the time of publication of this book. However, telephone area codes and business addresses may change over time.

General Supply Houses

BMI Supply
28 Logan Ave.
Glen Falls, NY 12801
(800) 836-0524

Designlab Chicago
806 N. Peoria Street
Chicago, IL 60622-5438
(312) 738-3305

Dudley Theatrical
4925 Harley Dr.
Walkertown, NC 27051
(800) 992-9871

McManus Enterprises
111 Union Ave.
Bala Cynwyd, PA 19004
(800) 523-0348

Mikan Theatricals
86 Tide Mill Road
Hampton, NH 03824
(800) BUY-MIKAN

Nelson Enterprises
1225 State Route 12,
Ste. 2
Frenchtown, NJ 08825
(908) 966-3939

Stageworks
1510 S. Main St.
Little Rock, AR 72202
(800) 888-1224

Syracuse Scenery and Stage
Lighting
101 Monarch Dr.
Liverpool, NY 13088
(800) 453-7775

Costumes and Masks

Alinco Costumes
5505 S. Riley Lane
Murray, UT 84107
(801) 266-6337

Associated Theatrical
Contractors
241 S. Union
Springfield, MO 65802
(417) 862-4725

Baxter-Gladrags Costume Co.
76 Essex St., 6th Floor
Boston, MA 02111
(617) 426-5494

Boston Costume
69 Kneeland St.
Boston, MA 02111
(617) 482-1632

Broadway Costumes, Inc.
954 W. Washington Blvd.
Chicago, IL 60607
(800) 397-3316

Center Stage Costumes and
Magic
3210 SW 35th Boulevard
Butler Plaza, Archer Rd.
Gainesville, FL 32608
(888) 331-0798

Costume Associates
702 E. McBee
Greenville, SC 29601
(803) 271-4260

Costume Holiday House
3038 Hayes Ave.
Fremont, OH 43420
(800) 348-6616

The Costumer
1020-1030 Barrett St.
Schenectady, NY 12305
(518) 374-7442

Costumes by Patti Jo
2339 5th Ave.
Moline, IL 61265
(309) 762-1013

Costumes by Pierre
1113 Walnut St.
Philadelphia, PA 19107
(800) 466-1395

Costumes Creative
9168 Brookville Rd.
Silver Spring, MD 20910
(301) 587-6275

Costumes Unlimited
3328 Edgewater Dr.
Orlando FL 32804
(800) 726-6275

Costume Zoo
12507 Sunset Ave.
Ocean City, MD 21842
(410)-213-0000

The Emperor's New Clothes
1503 2nd Ave. West
Seattle, WA 98119
(206) 282-8878
(specialty—Victorian)

Fantasy Festival Costume
432 Virginia St. Rt. 14
Crystal Lake, IL 60014
(773) 777-0222

Fantasy Headquarters
4065 N. Milwaukee Ave.
Chicago, IL 60641
(800) BUY-WIGS

Frankel's Costume Co.
4815 Fannin St.
Houston, TX 77004
(800) 848-0155

Fullerton Civic Light Opera Co.
218 W. Commonwealth Ave.
Fullerton, CA 92632
(714) 879-9716

Graight's Costumes
1120 SW 16th St., Ste. 7
Renton, WA 98055
(206) 226-2000

Hatcrafters, Inc.
20 N. Springfield Rd.
Clifton Heights, PA 19018
(610) 623-2620

Ibsen Costume Gallery
4981 Hamilton
Omaha, NE 68132
(800) 456-6938

Mecca Magic, Inc.
49 Dodd St.
Bloomfield, NJ 07003
(800) 732-1153

Mikan Theatricals
86 Tide Mill Road
Hampton, NH 03824
(800) BUY-MIKAN

Miller-Armstrong Costume
  Service
223 North Water Street
Milwaukee, WI 53202
(800) 657-0743

Mr. Fun's Costumes
3505 Wyoga Road
Cuyahoga Falls, OH 44224
(330) 923-3339

National Discount Costume
4901 Pacific Hwy.
San Diego, CA 92110
(619) 491-0030

Norcostco–California
3606 Magnolia Blvd.
Burbank, CA 91601-1035
(800) 220-6928

Norcostco–Denver
137 W. 10th Ave.
Denver, CO 80204
(800) 220-6928

Norcostco–Eastern
333A Route 46 West
Fairfield, NJ 07004-2442
(800) 220-6940

Norcostco–Northwestern
3203 N. Highway 100
Minneapolis, MN 55422
(800) 620-6920

Norcostco–Southeast
2089 Monroe Drive NE
Atlanta, GA 30324-4891
(800) 241-5356

Norcostco–Texas
1231 Wycliff Ave.
Suite 300
Dallas, TX 75207-6205
(800) 657-1887

Past Patterns
P. O. Box 2446
Richmond, IN 47375-2446
(765) 962-3773

Pierre's Costumes
Central Hwy. and Browning Rd.
Pennsauken, NJ 08110
(609) 486-1188

Production Values, Inc.
331 Elizabeth Street NE
Atlanta, GA 30307
(404) 584-5229

Raleigh's Creative Costumes
616 St. Mary's St.
Raleigh, NC 27609
(919) 834-4041

Robert Schmidt Costumes, Inc.
5411 Virginia Ave.
St. Louis, MO 63111
(314) 832-6800

S. A. Feather Co.
5852 Enterprise Parkway
Fort Myers, FL 33905
(800) 226-8698

Salt Lake Costume Co.
1701 South 11th East
Salt Lake City, UT 84105
(800) 467-9494

Schenz Theatrical Supply
2959 Colerain Ave.
Cincinnati, OH 45225-2103
(513) 542-6100

Scott Costume Co.
114 4th Street NW
Canton, OH 44702
(216) 452-6612

Shrader Bootmaker
San Anselmo, CA 94960
(415) 459-6576

Stage Door Costumes
14 Walnut Street
Peabody, MA 01960
(508) 531-7672

Stages
1132 Main Street
Wheeling, WV 26003
(304) 232-1107

Stitch-N-Tyme
14 West Delaware
Evansville, IN 47710
(812) 423-0238

The Theatre Company
687D North Benson Ave.
Upland, CA 91786
(714) 982-5736

Theatrics Unlimited
19 Magnolia Road
Charleston, SC 29407
(800) 758-7496

Tobins Lake Studio
7030 Old US 23
Brighton, MI 48116
(313) 299-6667

Tuxedo Wholesaler
7750 E. Redfield Rd., Ste. 103
Scottsdale, AZ 85260
(602) 951-1606

Unnatural Resources (masks)
14 Forest Ave.
Caldwell, NJ 07006
(800) 992-5540

Dancewear

All That Dance
160 Deer Park Ave.
Babylon, NY 11702
(516) 587-4549

Baum's, Inc.
106-114 South 11th St.
Philadelphia, PA 19107
(800) 832-6246

Capezio Ballet Makers, Inc.
1411 Broadway, 28th Floor
New York, NY 10018
(212) 354-1887

Costume Gallery
1604 South Route 130
Burlington, NJ 08016
(800) 222-8125

Curtain Call Costumes
333 East 7th Ave.
P. O. Box 709
York, PA 17405-0709
(717) 852-6910

The Dance Shop
2485 Forest Park Blvd.
Fort Worth, TX 76110
(800) 22-DANCE

Elite Sportswear, Ltd.
1230 Spruce St.
Reading, PA 19602
(800) 345-4087

Illinois Theatrical Co.
P. O. Box 34284
Chicago, IL 60634-0284
(312) 745-7777

Lebos, Inc.
4118 East Independence Blvd.
Charlotte, NC 28205
(704) 535-5000

MBA Productions
245–247 8th St., Suite 201
Jersey City, NJ 07302
(212) 262-0045

N Motion
c/o Nancy E. Fountain
2548 Ridgewood Ave.
Louisville, KY 40217
(502) 635-7701

The Red Shoes
1014 Mission St.
South Pasadena, CA 91030
(818) 799-8615

Star Styled Dancing Supplies
487 NW 42nd Ave.
Miami, FL 33126
(305) 649-3030

Trep-Art Theatrical
1932 East Park Place
Milwaukee, WI 53211
(414) 961-1125

Universal Dance Supply, Inc.
357 Grove St.
San Francisco, CA 94102
(415) 626-2099

Drapes, Drops, and Fabrics

A. E. Mitchell and Co.
6718 Princess Anne Lane
Falls Church, VA 22042
(703) 922-8810

Black Sheep Enterprises
9858 Glenoaks Blvd.
Sun Valley, CA 91352
(818) 767-7556

BMI Supply
28 Logan Ave.
Glen Falls, NY 12801
(800) 836-0524

Charles H. Stewart & Co.
P. O. Box 187
Somerville, MA 02144
(617) 625-2407

Design Source International
13201 NE 16th Ave.
North Miami, FL 33161
(305) 893-3430

Dudley Theatrical
4925 Harley Dr.
P. O. Box 519
Walkertown, NC 27051
(919) 595-2122

Fox-Rich Textiles, Inc.
54 Danbury Road, Ste. 228
Ridgefield, CT 06877
(914) 533-2445

Fullerton Civic Light Opera Co.
218 W. Commonwealth Ave.
Fullerton, CA 92632
(714) 879-9716

Gerriets International
R. D. #1
950 Hutchinson Road
Allentown, NJ 08501
(609) 758-9121

Grand Stage Company
620 West Lake Street
Chicago, IL 60661
(800) 621-2181

Grosh Scenic Studios
4114 Sunset Blvd.
Hollywood, CA 90029
(213) 662-1134

Joseph C. Hansen Co.
423 W. 43rd St.
New York, NY 10036
(212) 246-8055

Kenney Drapery Associates
13201 NE 16th Ave.
North Miami, FL 33161
(305) 895-2224

Leavitt & Parris, Inc.
448 Payne Road
P. O. Box 621
Scarborough, ME 04070
(207) 883-4184

Limelight Productions, Inc.
Route 102
Lee, MA 01238
(800) 243-4950

Madison, Inc.
1823 E. Venango Street
Philadelphia, PA 19134
(215) 535-2005

McManus Enterprises
111 Union Ave.
Bala Cynwyd, PA 19004
(800) 523-0348

Mikan Theatricals
86 Tide Mill Road
Hampton, NH 03824
(800) BUY-MIKAN

Musson Theatrical Inc.
5000 Crittenden Dr.
P. O. Box 9526
Louisville, KY 40209
(800) 852-6016

Nelson Enterprises
1225 State Route 12, Ste. 2
Frenchtown, NJ 08825
(908) 996-3939

Norcostco
3203 N. Highway 100
Minneapolis, MN 55422
(612) 533-2791
(for other locations, see listing
   under Costumes and Masks)

The Production Advantage
17 Pine Haven Shore
Shelburne, VT 05482
(800) 424-9991

Rose Brand Theatrical Fabrics
517 West 35th St.
New York, NY 10001
(800) 233-1624

Stageworks
1510 South Main Street
Little Rock, AR 72202
(800) 888-1224

Tobins Lake Studios
7030 Old US 23
Brighton, MI 48116
(313) 229-6667

Triangle
1215 Bates Ave.
Los Angeles, CA 90029
(213) 662-8129

Effects: Fog, Sound, Magic

Alcone Co.
5–49 49th Ave.
Long Island City, NY 11101
(718) 361-8373

Associated Theatrical
 Contractors (fog)
307 W. 80th
Kansas City, MO 64114
(816) 523-1655

Bay Stage Lighting Co.
310 S. MacDil Ave.
Tampa, FL 33609
(813) 877-1089

Burman Industries
14141 Covello St., #6-A
Van Nuys, CA 91405
(818) 782-9833

Kamar Products, Inc.
 (mirrors, rear projection)
P. O. Box 227
Irvington, NY 10533
(914) 591-8700

Kinetic Artistry (fog)
7216 Carroll Ave.
Takoma Park, MD 20912
(800) 444-0411

Mecca Magic, Inc.
49 Dodd St.
Bloomfield, NJ 07003
(201) 429-7597

Radio Systems, Inc. (sound)
P. O. Box 458
Bridgeport, NJ 08014
(609) 467-8000

Stage Step (sound tracks)
P. O. Box 328
Philadelphia, PA 19105
(800) 523-0960

Twin Cities Magic and Costume
241 West Seventh St.
St. Paul, MN 55102
(612) 227-7888

Lighting Equipment and Supplies

Alcone Co. Inc.
5–49 49th Ave.
Long Island City, NY 11101
(718) 361-8373

Associated Theatrical
 Contractors
307 West 80th
Kansas City, MO 64114
(816) 523-1655

Bairstow Distributing Co.
1785 Ellsworth Industrial Dr.
Atlanta, GA 30318
(800) 241-8990

Bay Stage Lighting Co.
310 S. MacDil Ave.
Tampa, FL 33609
(813) 877-1089

BMI Supply
28 Logan Ave.
Glen Falls, NY 12801
(800) 836-0524

Designlab Chicago
806 N. Peoria St.
Chicago, IL 60622-5438
(312) 738-3305

Dudley Theatrical
4925 Harley Dr.
P. O. Box 519
Walkertown, NC 27051
(919) 595-2122

Globe Theatrical Supply
813 Pearl St.
Sioux City, IA 51101-1040
(712) 255-0972

Grand Stage Co.
630 West Lake St.
Chicago, IL 60661
(800) 621-2181

The Great American Market
826 N. Cole Ave.
Hollywood, CA 90038
(213) 461-0200

High Output, Inc.
184 Everett St.
Boston, MA 02134
(617) 787-4747

JCN Computer Technology
P. O. Box 9986
Oakland, CA 94613
(510) 638-6907

Kinetic Artistry
7216 Carroll Ave.
Takoma Park, MD 20912
(800) 444-0411

Kliegl Bros.
5 Aerial Way
Syosset, NY 11791-5502
(516) 937-3900

Little Stage Lighting Co.
10507 Harry Hines Blvd.
Dallas, TX 75220
(214) 358-3511

Magnum Companies
170-A Ottley Dr. NE
Atlanta, GA 30324
(800) 255-1774

McManus Enterprises
111 Union Ave.
Bala Cynwyd, PA 19004
(800) 523-0348

Mid-West Scenic & Stage
  Equipment Co.
224 West Bruce Street
Milwaukee, WI 53204
(800) 43-STAGE

Musson Theatrical, Inc.
5000 Crittenden Dr.
P. O. Box 9526
Louisville, KY 40209
(800) 852-6016

Nelson Enterprises
1225 State Route 12, Ste. 2
Frenchtown, NJ 08825
(908) 996-3939

Norcostco
4203 N. Highway 100
Minneapolis, MN 55422
(612) 533-2791
(for other locations, see listings
  under Costumes and Masks)

Olesen
1535 Ivar Ave.
Hollywood, CA 90028
(800) 821-1656

Paragon Productions, Inc.
720 Old Friendship Road
Rock Hill, SC 29730
(803) 329-3939

PNTA
333 Westlake Ave. North
Seattle, WA 98109
(800) 622-7850

The Production Advantage
17 Pine Haven Shore
Shelburne, VT 05482
(800) 424-9991

Rosco Laboratories, Inc.
36 Bush Ave.
Port Chester, NY 10573
(914) 937-1300

Sanders Lighting Templates
5830 West Patterson Ave.
Chicago, IL 60634-2680
(773) 736-9551

SECOA
2731 Nevada Ave. North
Minneapolis, MN 55427
(800) 328-5519

Sitler's Supplies
P. O. Box 10
Washington, IA 52353
(800) 426-3938

SLD Lighting
318 West 47th St.
New York, NY 10036
(800) 245-6630

Sunshine Productions
2015 6th Ave. North
Great Falls, MT 59401
(406) 452-0307

Syracuse Scenery & Stage
  Lighting Co.
101 Monarch Dr.
Liverpool, NY 13088
(800) 453-7775

United Stage Associates
97 Liberty Ave.
New Rochelle, NY 10805
(914) 633-8550

Makeup and Wigs

Alcone Co.
5–49 49th Ave.
Long Island City, NY 11101
(718) 361-8373

Associated Theatrical
  Contractors
307 W. 80th
Kansas City, MO 64114
(816) 523-1655

Backstage
41 West Broadway
Eugene, OR 97401
(800) 882-4888

Baum's, Inc.
106–114 S. 11th St.
Philadelphia, PA 19107
(800) 832-6246

Ben Nye Makeup
5935 Bowcraft St.
Los Angeles, CA 90016
(310) 839-1984

Boston Costume Co.
69 Kneeland St.
Boston, MA 02111
(617) 482-1632

Burman Industries, Inc.
14141 Covello St., #6-A
Van Nuys, CA 91405
(818) 782-9833

Costume Holiday House
3038 Hayes Ave.
Fremont, OH 43420
(800) 348-6616

The Costumer
1020–1030 Barrett St.
Schenectady, NY 12305
(518) 374-7442

Costumes by Patti Jo
2339 5th Ave.
Moline, IL 61265
(309) 762-1013

Costumes by Pierre
1113 Walnut St.
Philadelphia, PA 19107
(800) 466-1395

Costumes Creative
9168 Brookville Rd.
Silver Spring, MD 20910
(301) 587-6275

Dudley Theatrical
4925 Harley Dr.
P. O. Box 519
Walkertown, NC 27051
(919) 595-2122

Fantasy Festival Costume
432 Virginia St., Rt. 14
Crystal Lake, IL 60014
(815) 455-4910

Fantasy Headquarters
4065 N. Milwaukee Ave.
Chicago, IL 60641
(800) USA-WIGS

Frankel's Costume Co.
4815 Fannin St.
Houston, TX 77004
(800) 848-0155

Globe Theatrical Supply
813 Pearl St.
Sioux City, IA 51101-1040
(712) 255-0972

Grand Stage Company
630 West Lake St.
Chicago, IL 60661
(800) 621-2181

Ibsen Costume Gallery
4981 Hamilton
Omaha, NE 68132
(800) 456-6938

Ideal Wig Co.
37-11 35th Ave.
Astoria, NY 11101
(718) 361-8601

Jack Stein Makeup Center
186 South St.
Boston, MA 02111
(800) 562-3217

Joe Blasco Cosmetics
7340 Greenbriar Parkway
Orlando, FL 32819
(800) 553-1520

Kinetic Artistry
7216 Carroll Ave.
Takoma Park, MD 20912
(800) 444-0411

Lacey Costume Wig
249 West 34th St., #707
New York, NY 10001
(800) 562-9911

Little Stage Lighting Co.
10507 Harry Hines Blvd.
Dallas, TX 75220
(214) 358-3511

McManus Enterprises
111 Union Ave.
Bala Cynwyd, PA 19004
(800) 523-0348

Mecca Magic
49 Dodd St.
Bloomfield, NJ 07003
(201) 429-7597

Mehron, Inc.
45E Route 303
Valley Cottage, NY 10989
(914) 268-4106

Miller-Armstrong Costume
  Service
223 North Water St.
Milwaukee, WI 53202
(800) 657-0743

Mr. Fun's Costumes
3505 Wyoga Rd.
Cuyahoga Falls, OH 44224
(216) 923-3339

Raleigh Creative Costumes
616 St. Mary's St.
Raleigh, NC 27609
(919) 834-4041

Robert Schmidt Costumes
5411 Virginia Ave.
St. Louis, MO 63111
(314) 832-6800

Salt Lake Costume Co.
1701 South 11th East
Salt Lake City, UT 84105
(800) 467-9494

Schenz Theatrical Supply
2959 Colerain Ave.
Cincinnati, OH 45225
(800) 435-7013

Scott Costume Co. (wigs)
114 4th St. NW
Canton, OH 44702
(216) 452-6612

Stage Door Costumes
14 Walnut St.
Peabody, MA 01960
(508) 531-7262

Stages
1132 Main St.
Wheeling, WV 26003
(304) 232-1107

Stageworks, Inc.
1510 S. Main St.
Little Rock, AR 72202
(800) 888-1224

Stein Cosmetic Co.
10 Henry St.
Freeport, NY 11520
(516) 379-2600

Stitch-N-Tyme
14 W. Delaware
Evansville, IN 47710
(812) 423-0238

Syracuse Scenery and Stage
  Lighting
101 Monarch Dr.
Liverpool, NY 13088
(800) 453-7775

Theatrics Unlimited
19 Magnolia Road
Charleston, SC 29407
(800) 255-0038

Twin Cities Magic and Costume
241 West Seventh St.
St. Paul, MN 55102
(612) 227-7888

Vermont Theatrical Supply
8 Diane Drive
Colchester, VT 05446
(802) 655-4777

Paint*

Alcone Company
5–49 49th Ave.
Long Island City, NY 11101
(718) 361-8373

BMI Supply
28 Logan Ave.
Glen Falls, NY 12801
(800) 836-0524

Designlab Chicago
806 N. Peoria Street
Chicago, IL 60622-5438
(312) 738-3305

Dudley Theatrical
4925 Harley Dr.
P. O. Box 519
Walkertown, NC 27051
(919) 595-2122

Kinetic Artistry
7216 Carroll Ave.
Takoma Park, MD 20912
(800) 444-0411

McManus Enterprises
111 Union Ave.
Bala Cynwyd, PA 19004
(800) 523-0348

Mikan Theatricals
86 Tide Mill Road
Hampton, NH 03824
(800) BUY-MIKAN

Norcostco
3203 N. Highway 100
Minneapolis, MN 55422
(612) 533-2791
(for other locations see listings
  under Costumes and Masks)

Rosco
36 Bush Ave.
Port Chester, NY 10573
(914) 937-1300

*Check with local paint
suppliers for casein colors.*

Periodicals

Back Stage Publications, Inc.
330 West 42nd Street
New York, NY 10036
(212) 947-0020

Drama-Logue
P. O. Box 38771
Hollywood, CA 90038
(213) 464-5079

Performing Arts Forum
P. O. Box 200328
Austin, TX 78720
(512) 346-1328

Performing Arts Journal
131 Varick St., Suite 902
New York, NY 10013
(212) 243-3885

Stage Directions
3020 Beacon Blvd.
West Sacramento, CA 95691-
  3436
(916) 373-0201

Theatre Crafts
135 5th Ave.
New York, NY 10010-7193

Theatre Design and Technology
10 West 19th St., Suite 5A
New York, NY 10011-4206
(212) 924-9088

Props

Charles H. Stewart & Co.
P. O. Box 187
Somerville, MA 02144
(617) 625-2407

Collector's Armoury (replica
  guns, swords, armour)
800 Slaters Lane
P. O. Box 59
Alexandria, VA 22313
(703) 684-6111

Cumberland Co.
P. O. Box 7428
Cumberland, RI 02864
(401) 333-9000

Old Telephones (rental)
207 East Mill Road
Galesville, WI 54630
(608) 582-4124

Unnatural Resources
 (thermoplastics)
14 Forest Ave.
Caldwell, NJ 07006
(800) 992-5540

Publicity

Baker's Plays (posters)
100 Chauncy St.
Boston, MA 02111-1783
(617) 482-1280

Broadway Button (buttons and
 T-shirts)
88 Bleecker St. #2H
New York, NY 10012
(800) 869-9894

Dramatic Publishing Co.
 (posters)
P. O. Box 129
311 Washington St.
Woodstock, IL 60098
(800) HIT-SHOW

Fogels Design and Photography
28 Mugford St.
Marblehead, MA 01945
(617) 639-0195

Package Publicity Service
 (posters)
27 West 24th St., Ste. 402
New York, NY 10010
(800) 882-9774

Rigging and Hardware

A. E. Mitchell & Co.
6718 Princess Anne Lane
Falls Church, VA 22042
(703) 922-8810

Associated Theatrical
 Contractors
307 West 80th
Kansas City, MO 64114
(816) 523-1655

Bairstow Distributing Co.
1785 Ellsworth Industrial Dr.
Atlanta, GA 30318
(800) 241-8990

Dudley Theatrical
4925 Harley Dr.
P. O. Box 519
Walkertown, NC 27051
(919) 595-2122

Grosh Scenic Studios
4114 Sunset Blvd.
Hollywood, CA 90029
(213) 662-1134

Joseph C. Hansen Co.
423 West 43rd St.
New York, NY 10036
(212) 246-8055

Kenney Drapery
13201 NE 16th Ave.
North Miami, FL 33161
(800) 543-1842

Limelight Productions, Inc.
Route 102
Lee, MA 01238
(800) 243-4950

Madison, Inc.
1823 East Venango St.
Philadelphia, PA 19134
(215) 535-2005

McManus Enterprises
111 Union Ave.
Bala Cynwyd, PA 19004
(800) 523-0348

The Production Advantage
17 Pine Haven Shore
Shelburne, VT 05482
(800) 424-9991

Sapsis Rigging, Inc.
233 N. Lansdowne Ave.
Lansdowne, PA 19050
(215) 849-6660

Syracuse Scenery & Stage
 Lighting
101 Monarch Dr.
Liverpool, NY 10036
(800) 453-7775

Scenery Construction and Rental

Charles H. Stewart & Co.
P. O. Box 187
Somerville, MA 02144
(617) 625-2407

Fullerton Civic Light Opera Co.
218 W. Commonwealth Ave.
Fullerton, CA 92632
(714) 879-9716

JNC Computer Technology
P. O. Box 9986
Oakland, CA 94613
(510) 638-6907

ShowBiz Enterprises
15541 Lanark St.
Van Nuys, CA 91406
(800) 746-9249

Technique, Inc.
1530 Custer Ave.
San Francisco, CA 94124
(415) 824-7444

Sound Equipment

Baker's Plays (sound effects)
100 Chauncy St.
Boston, MA 02111-1783
(617) 482-7613

Bose Corp.
The Mountain Rd.
Framingham, MA 01701
(617) 879-7330

The Dramatic Publishing Co.
 (sound effects)
P. O. Box 129
311 Washington St.
Woodstock, IL 60098
(800) HIT-SHOW

Dudley Theatrical
 (intercoms and headsets)
4925 Harley Dr.
P. O. Box 519
Walkertown, NC 27051
(919) 595-2122

Erskine-Shapiro Theatre
 Technology, Inc.
37 West 20th St.
New York, NY 10011
(212) 929-5380

Grand Stage Co. (intercoms
 and headsets)
630 West Lake St.
Chicago, IL 60661
(800) 621-2181

Kinetic (intercoms and headsets)
7216 Carroll Ave.
Takoma Park, MD 20912
(800) 444-0411

McManus Enterprises
111 Union Ave.
Bala Cynwyd, PA 19004
(800) 523-0348

Paragon Productions, Inc.
720 Old Friendship Rd.
Rock Hill, SC 29730
(803) 329-3939

Radio Systems, Inc.
P. O. Box 458
Bridgeport, NJ 08014
(609) 467-8000

Sescom, Inc.
2100 Ward Dr.
Henderson, NV 89015-4249
(702) 565-3400

Sunshine Productions
2015 6th Ave. North
Great Falls, MT 59401
(406) 452-0307

Resources

████████████████████████████████████

In grades 9–12, students view and construct dramatic works as metaphorical visions of life that embrace connotative meanings, juxtaposition, ambiguity, and varied interpretations. By creating, performing, analyzing, and critiquing dramatic performances, they develop a deeper understanding of personal issues and a broader worldview that includes global issues. Since theatre in all its forms reflects and affects life, students should learn about representative dramatic texts and performances and the place of that work and those events in history. Classroom work becomes more formalized with the advanced students participating in theatre, film, television, and electronic media productions.

1. **Content Standard:** Script writing through improvising, writing, and refining scripts based on personal experience and heritage, imagination, literature, and history

Achievement Standard, Proficient:
Students
   a. construct imaginative scripts and collaborate with actors to refine scripts so that story and meaning are conveyed to an audience

Achievement Standard, Advanced:
Students
   b. write theatre, film, television, or electronic media scripts in a variety of traditional and new forms that include original characters with unique dialogue that motivates action

2. **Content Standard:** Acting by developing, communicating, and sustaining characters in improvisations and informal or formal productions

Achievement Standard, Proficient:
Students

   a. analyze the physical, emotional, and social dimensions of characters found in dramatic texts from various genres and media

   b. compare and demonstrate various classical and contemporary acting techniques and methods

   c. in an ensemble, create and sustain characters that communicate with audiences

Achievement Standard, Advanced:

Students

    d. demonstrate artistic discipline to achieve an ensemble in rehearsal and performance

    e. create consistent characters from classical, contemporary, realistic, and nonrealistic dramatic texts in informal and formal theatre, film, television, or electronic media productions

    3. Content Standard: Designing and producing by conceptualizing and realizing artistic interpretations for informal or formal productions

Achievement Standard, Proficient:

Students

    a. explain the basic physical and chemical properties of the technical aspects of theatre (such as light, color, electricity, paint, and makeup)

    b. analyze a variety of dramatic texts from cultural and historical perspectives to determine production requirements

    c. develop designs that use visual and aural elements to convey environments that clearly support the text

    d. apply technical knowledge and skills to collaboratively and safely create functional scenery, properties, lighting, sound, costumes, and makeup

    e. design coherent stage management, promotional, and business plans

Achievement Standard, Advanced:

Students

    f. explain how scientific and technological advances have impacted set, light, sound, and costume design and implementation for theatre, film, television, and electronic media productions

    g. collaborate with directors to develop unified production concepts that convey the metaphorical nature of the drama for informal and formal theatre, film, television, or electronic media productions

    h. safely construct and efficiently operate technical aspects of theatre, film, television, or electronic media productions

    i. create and reliably implement production schedules, stage management plans, promotional ideas, and business and front of house procedures for informal and formal theatre, film, television, or electronic media productions

    4. Content Standard: Directing by interpreting dramatic texts and organizing and conducting rehearsals for informal or formal productions

Achievement Standard, Proficient:

Students

    a. develop multiple interpretations and visual and aural production choices for scripts and production ideas and choose those that are most interesting

    b. justify selections of text, interpretation, and visual and aural artistic choices

    c. effectively communicate directorial choices to a small ensemble for improvised or scripted scenes

Achievement Standard, Advanced:

Students

    d. explain and compare the roles and interrelated responsibilities of the various personnel involved in theatre, film, television, and electronic media productions

    e. collaborate with designers and actors to develop aesthetically unified production concepts for informal and formal theatre, film, television, or electronic media productions

    f. conduct auditions, cast actors, direct scenes, and conduct production meetings to achieve production goals

5. **Content Standard:** Researching by evaluating and synthesizing cultural and historical information to support artistic choices

Achievement Standard, Proficient:

Students

    a. identify and research cultural, historical, and symbolic clues in dramatic texts, and evaluate the validity and practicality of the information to assist in making artistic choices for informal and formal productions

Achievement Standard, Advanced:

Students

    b. research and describe appropriate historical production designs, techniques, and performances from various cultures to assist in making artistic choices for informal and formal theatre, film, television, or electronic media productions

6. **Content Standard:** Comparing and integrating art forms by analyzing traditional theatre, dance, music, visual arts, and new art forms

Achievement Standard, Proficient:

Students

    a. describe and compare the basic nature, materials, elements, and means of communicating in theatre, dramatic media, musical theatre, dance, music, and the visual arts

    b. determine how the nondramatic art forms are modified to enhance the expression of ideas and emotions in theatre

c. illustrate the integration of several arts media in informal presentations

Achievement Standard, Advanced:
Students

d. compare the interpretive and expressive natures of several art forms in a specific culture or historical period

e. compare the unique interpretive and expressive natures and aesthetic qualities of traditional arts from various cultures and historical periods with contemporary new art forms (such as performance art)

f. integrate several arts and/or media in theatre, film, television, or electronic media productions

7. **Content Standard:** Analyzing, critiquing, and constructing meanings from informal and formal theatre, film, television, and electronic media productions

Achievement Standard, Proficient:
Students

a. construct social meanings from informal and formal productions and from dramatic performances from a variety of cultures and historical periods, and relate these to current personal, national, and international issues

b. articulate and justify personal aesthetic criteria for critiquing dramatic texts and events that compare perceived artistic intent with the final aesthetic achievement

c. analyze and critique the whole and the parts of dramatic performances, taking into account the context, and constructively suggest alternative artistic choices

d. constructively evaluate their own and others' collaborative efforts and artistic choices in informal and formal productions

Achievement Standard, Advanced:
Students

e. construct personal meanings from nontraditional dramatic performances

f. analyze, compare, and evaluate differing critiques of the same dramatic texts and performances

g. critique several dramatic works in terms of other aesthetic philosophies (such as the underlying ethos of Greek drama, French classicism with its unities of time and place, Shakespeare and romantic forms, India classical drama, Japanese Kabuki, and others)

h. analyze and evaluate critical comments about personal dramatic work explaining which points are most appropriate to inform further development of the work

8. **Content Standard:** Understanding context by analyzing the role of theatre, film, television, and electronic media in the past and the present

Achievement Standard, Proficient:

Students

  a. compare how similar themes are treated in drama from various cultures and historical periods, illustrate with informal performances, and discuss how theatre can reveal universal concepts

  b. identify and compare the lives, works, and influence of representative theatre artists in various cultures and historical periods

  c. identify cultural and historical sources of American theatre and musical theatre

  d. analyze the effect of their own cultural experiences on their dramatic work

Achievement Standard, Advanced:

Students

  e. analyze the social and aesthetic impact of underrepresented theatre and film artists

  f. analyze the relationships among cultural values, freedom of artistic expression, ethics, and artistic choices in various cultures and historical periods

  g. analyze the development of dramatic forms, production practices, and theatrical traditions across cultures and historical periods and explain influences on contemporary theatre, film, television, and electronic media productions